THE QUALITY OF WORKING LIFE
AND THE 1980s

THE QUALITY OF WORKING LIFE AND THE 1980s

Edited by
Harvey Kolodny and Hans van Beinum

PRAEGER SPECIAL STUDIES • PRAEGER SCIENTIFIC

Library of Congress Cataloging in Publication Data
Main entry under title:

The Quality of working life in the 1980s.

    Bibliography: p.
    Includes index.
    1. Quality of work life—Congresses. I. Kolodny,
Harvey. II. Beinum, Hans van, 1926–
HD4813.Q34 1983 658.3'142   83-9495
ISBN 0-03-063342-7

Published in 1983 by Praeger Publishers
CBS Educational and Professional Publishing
A Division of CBS, Inc.
521 Fifth Avenue, New York, New York 10175 U.S.A.

© 1983 by Praeger Publishers

3456789   052   987654321

Printed in the United States of America on acid-free paper.

This book is dedicated to the members of the Steering Committee who made the Toronto conference, QWL and the 80's possible.

Steering Committee

Hugh Auld, *Smith, Auld & Associates, Canada*
Norm Bromberger, *Saskatchewan Credit Union Central, Canada*
Doug Brown, *retired, Canadian General Electric Canada*
Don Bryant, *B.C. Research, Canada*
Albert Cherns, *Loughborough University, England*
Max Clarkson, *University of Toronto, Canada*
John Dougall, *Dalhousie University, Canada*
Carl Johnston, *Air Canada, Canada*
Harvey Kolodny, *University of Toronto, Canada (Coordinator)*
Maurice Lemelin, *Ecole des Hautes Etudes Commerciales, Canada*
Jack Levine, *Steinberg Inc., Canada*
Rod MacLeod, *Labour Canada, Canada*
Denise Moncion, *Heritage, Canada*
Bert Painter, *B.C. Research, Canada*
Norm Paxton, *retired, Canadian Paper Workers Union, Canada*
Denis Sexton, *United Food and Commercial Workers, Canada*
Stanley Surma, *Ford Motor Company of Canada Ltd., Canada*
James Taylor, *University of California (Los Angeles), and Consultant, U.S.A.*
Robert Taylor, *Shell Canada Ltd., Canada*
Eric Trist, *York University, Canada/University of Pennsylvania (Wharton School), U.S.A.*
Hans van Beinum, *Ontario QWL Centre, Canada (Coordinator)*
William Westley, *McGill University, Canada*
Terry White, *University of Alberta, Canada*

Preface

In 1972 an international conference took place at Arden House, New York. This conference was attended by about 60 people, mainly academics, and dealt with the practice and theory of the democratization of work. The timing was right, and the event was clearly a success: more than a decade of European and American experiences were pooled; the term "quality of working life" was born; the International Council for the Quality of Working Life was established; and within a few years two important volumes of papers, edited by Louis Davis and Albert Cherns, were produced.

1972 became a punctuation point in the history of the quality of working life (QWL). Since then many developments have taken place; conceptual ones, methodological ones, and, more significantly, developments in the actual practice of organizing and reorganizing work. Major innovative work has been undertaken, not only in Europe and North America, but also in such places as India and, particularly, Australia.

In 1980 some members of the International Council for the Quality of Working Life suggested that it was time to have another international conference. Canada looked like the right place to host such an event. QWL developments in Canada were gaining momentum. Furthermore, it seemed that the Canadian environment could accommodate both the European and the U.S. traditions and developments.

In May 1980 about 30 representatives from labor, management, government, and academia from across Canada were invited to a weekend meeting in Toronto in order to discuss the International Council's proposal. At this meeting the idea of a conference was warmly received and an organizing body for such a conference was established. With the theme and the title "QWL and the 80s/la QVT et les années 80," the first open international conference took place in Toronto in August, 1981. This book arises directly out of that conference.

The 1981 conference was clearly a repunctuation point. A very significant development had taken place; the field had shifted. The Toronto conference demonstrated that QWL is no longer the exclusive concern of academics but is becoming more and more an issue of ongoing organizational reality.

Many different aspects of the conference program served to attract participants from more than 20 countries to Toronto. Central among them were the seven keynote speakers. Each is a pioneer in the quality of working life field, a field that is at the leading edge of a new paradigm of work.

While the past contributions of these keynote speakers are significant, their current contributions are equally important. Each continues to be actively involved in explaining the world of work and the relationships of people to their organizational and environmental contexts. They are still breaking new ground, and their current thoughts provide a vital continuity in the history of the field. Their conference presentations are included here. However, the printed texts of each "talk" have been elaborated beyond the presentations given.

David Jenkins's chapter sets the QWL 80's Conference in perspective. Calling on his familiarity with European experience, he related the presentations at the conference to the progress of the field both in Europe and North America. His overview provides an insightful introduction to the field and sets the papers that follow in a meaningful context.

Irving Bluestone's chapter follows. He has been an articulate and courageous spokesman for organized labor and is acutely aware of the need to find avenues of management and labor cooperation beyond the traditional collective bargaining agreement. It was his early and clear voice that provided an example to many leaders, on both the union and management sides, to take up the challenge of finding a new way to make work more dignified and more effective.

Eric Trist's address closed the conference. With Fred Emery, his conceptual contributions laid the foundations of the QWL field. He has had a particularly significant effect on the development of the quality of working life field in Canada, and the conference was honored to have him deliver the final address. His chapter reviews some of the differences in how we have come to regard work and how those attitudes toward the quality of working life are developing worldwide. It concludes by commenting on some of his current interests in advancing the quality of working life at the community or "macrosocietal" level.

Richard Walton's chapter addresses an area that he believes will be one of the most important in the 1980s. He has applied his considerable experience in the design of new plants to the area of advanced information technology or integrated office systems. His chapter identifies some critical areas where we can exercise "social choice" in the arrangement of work so that the undesirable social excesses of assembly line technology need not be repeated in the rapidly developing information technologies.

The chapter by Louis Davis summarizes years of experience in advising on the design of new organizations. The chapter provides detailed guidance in the design process, including the organization philosophy, the interface with the environment, the structure of the organization, the technical and social systems, and the related organizational building blocks. It is a welcome set of "learnings" from an eminent organization designer who was one of the first to flag the social failings of conventional production line technology.

Albert Cherns, in his chapter on the "state of the art" in QWL, draws on current experience to identify the forces that will effect the future meanings people will draw from their relationships at work and from a changing environment. He addresses changing work roles and changing societal values. While positive about current "QWL outcomes," he is more questioning about the meaning individuals will attach to future outcomes.

Einar Thorsrud's chapter provides concrete examples of how people advancing the QWL frontiers in one country have been able to learn from another country's experiences and have, in turn, shared their own experiences. Addressing the issue of international learning, he cites examples from international agencies, from multinational corporations, and from personal experience with an international seminar in the shipping industry that addressed the issue of sociotechnical design of new ships.

Fred Emery has been the quintessential theorist of a new paradigm of work. His classic articles with Eric Trist on sociotechnical systems and the causal texture of the environment, and his subsequent publications, *Futures We Are In* and *Choice of Futures*, with his wife Merrelyn Emery, had enormous impact on the field. His current work appears no less promising. Calling on Kondratiev's theory of long economic cycles, and developing a new educational paradigm to examine "the barriers between work, management and governance", he lays the foundations for a new social order.

Ann Armstrong attended as many sessions as she could at the conference and then listened to many of the others on tape. In her chapter, "Six Early Cases," she has selected a sample of cases that reflect the pragmatic orientation of much of the conference.

Our chapter, with Ann Armstrong, focuses specifically on the conference. Hopefully, it adds to David Jenkins's attempt to provide meaning and explanation.

We would also like to use this introduction to acknowledge the assistance of so many who made the conference a success, and particularly to the full-time conference staff, Patricia Lang, Jeannie Cohen, Sonia Grisonich, and Maria Reimer, all of whom remain involved with the field.

Toronto, July, 1982
Harvey Kolodny
Hans van Beinum

Contents

THE QUALITY OF WORKING LIFE AND THE 1980s

1
Quality of Working Life: Trends and Directions

David Jenkins

The following is a status report on activities, theories, and results, as reflected in the QWL and the 80s' Conference, held in Toronto, August 30–September 3, 1981. This chapter summarizes some of the major themes, viewpoints, and questions raised by the speakers and participants at the conference in the context of the events in the field during the recent past.

An unprecedented overview of the organization of work, its social, psychological, administrative, and technical aspects—how it's done, what's wrong with it, how it could and should be done—was delivered to the participants at the Toronto QWL and the 80s Conference.

By gathering together most of the leading authorities on the organization of work throughout the world and presenting a representative sampling of virtually all types of activities in this field, the conference made available, in highly concentrated form, most of what is now known about the subject. It thus provided an opportunity to size up the major trends and currents and probable developments over the coming years.

This brief chapter will focus on some highlights of the conference and, in so doing, supply a fast glimpse of the progress that has been made over the past several years. What follows is based on observations and comments made at the conference examined against the perspective of the preceding several years of rapid development and change.

TERMINOLOGY, DOCTRINES, AND MISCELLANEOUS DEFINITIONS

First, a note on terminology. The official concern of the conference was the quality of working life—a broad expression covering a vast variety of programs, techniques, theories, and management styles through which organ-

izations and jobs are designed so as to grant workers more autonomy, responsibility, and authority than is usually the case. To simplify somewhat,
the general objective is to arrange organizations, management procedures,
and jobs for the maximum utilization of individual talents and skills, in order to create more challenging and satisfying work and improve organizational effectiveness. The expression quality of working life (QWL) is sometimes used by various theorists to designate highly specific sets of theories
corresponding to certain philosophies or schools of thought—though different experts hold different opinions about what the correct doctrines are.
Most QWL specialists, particularly in North America, feel that the integration of feedback from the persons affected by a system in its design and
operations is a desirable and perhaps essential feature of QWL and that
"participation" is an increasingly natural element of work organizations.
Many theoreticians are interested in the finer gradation of meaning, but
most outside observers—and, indeed, most practitioners—are not.

As interest in the field has grown, QWL has come to be loosely used to
cover a broad spectrum of activities in this area. Other terms used in rough-
ly the same way as QWL include job design, organizational design, humanization of work, participative management, job reform, and work
structuring. Disagreements on definitions continue to irritate and confuse.
One specialist at the Toronto conference said of his company's human resources approach, "It is not talk about the quality of working life, but it is
talk about the business at hand and who's responsible for managing it." On
the whole, however, the above expressions are now employed as normal
and acceptable generic terms.

It can be added that all these expressions are often extended to cover
efforts to improve other aspects of workplace environments, such as ergo-
nomics, noise, lighting, and health and safety.

A DECADE OF CHANGE

It is only during the past ten years or so that QWL has become of sufficient
significance to be noticeable—and in some countries the time span has
been a good deal less than that. We will now examine the changes that have
occurred over that time period.

Most importantly, there has been an immense increase in the number
of persons interested in the subject. Only a few years ago the thought of organizing an event such as the Toronto conference would have seemed fool-
hardy, not to say useless. Previous meetings on QWL had taken the form of
small seminars or workshops mainly aimed at initiating newcomers to the
field, or moderately sized conferences designed for highly specialized professionals. The 1,700 participants at the Toronto conference comfortably

exceeded the sponsors' expectations. Significantly, about 1,000 of these were managers, and another 250 were from unions. As nearly as can be determined, they felt the conference would assist them in their day-to-day work. Ten years ago, only a handful of managers, and virtually no unionists, would have seen knowledge of QWL as fitting even remotely into their work.*

QWL as a Corporate Value

The enthusiastic response to the conference is, of course, a consequence of the inclusion of QWL as a top level management priority in a number of leading companies. Ten years ago (to mention three examples of companies that this writer happened to come across at the time), American Telephone and Telegraph (AT&T) and General Motors (GM) had small, semiexperimental QWL teams tucked away in obscure corners of their bureaucracies — with little attention being paid to their activities — and the Aluminum Corporation of America (Alcoa) was just then in the early, hesitant stages of entering QWL. Today job design and organizational improvement are seen as urgent and essential at AT&T and GM, and both companies have elicited the cooperation of unions in making sure the campaigns work. Alcoa has now designed several plants using QWL principles, and has reached agreement with unions on contractual specifications on the QWL objectives. More significantly, it is putting into place a new set of corporate goals that incorporate QWL thinking.

The seriousness with which these senior corporate managers take QWL is having a major effect on the thinking of smaller companies, consti tuting persuasive evidence that QWL is not merely one more fad, fashion, or empty management gizmo.

The Role of a QWL Consultant

The broadening of the field is also reflected in the variety of consultant services available. Ten years ago there were almost no consultants outside a handful of universities and research institutes, either in Europe or North America. Today numerous highly competent independent consultants with solid operating backgrounds in industrial companies that have pioneered in the QWL field are available. In fact, so hot is the demand for the insufficient number of people with QWL expertise that companies have begun to experience some difficulty in holding together their internal consulting staffs.

---

*The conference also attracted about 50 consultants, 300 persons from universities, 100 from governmental agencies, and a scattering of representatives of private research institutes and other miscellaneous bodies.

General Motors, for example, has recently lost a number of its people, so green have the pastures appeared elsewhere.

As practical experience in QWL has accumulated, valuable knowledge has been gained on the workings of the process — the results that may be expected and the common pitfalls that can be advantageously avoided. One useful lesson concerns the role of consultants. At one time external consultants were, and were so perceived by those at the site where they were working, as far better informed than their clients on the intricacies of their work. They exercised excessive control over their projects with the too frequent result that when the consultant disappeared, so did the QWL project. Most external consultants now emphasize that the project, the new organization, and the redesigned jobs, belong to those who are going to work in them — managers, supervisors, and operators — and strive to disconnect themselves as soon as those on the spot are able to take command. One frequent recommendation of the consultants is that an internal consulting resource be created.

It is now widely recognized that overprotection of QWL projects can be counterproductive. Many companies, understandably cautious in dealing with unfamiliar ideas, start QWL activities in a small department, carefully shielded from other units so that the process will not be disrupted and so that its effects may be observed. This is probably unavoidable, but if it is exaggerated, as has happened, considerable friction is built up between the trial area and other departments, leading to criticism, rivalry, and envy of the "pampered" unit being accorded special privileges. Consultants now encourage their clients to involve persons from adjacent units in any organizational change process to assure them that the project is in their long-run interests and thus win their support, and to spread the process to other sections as rapidly as possible to minimize the "special status" of any one department.

In other words, QWL experts — who urge their clients to regard a QWL process as a learning experience for individuals and organizations — have engaged in fruitful learning experiences themselves. As a result, projects can now get off the ground more quickly than in the past. Many of those involved still feel that excessive amounts of patience and hard work are needed to get airborne, but in the past many projects dragged on for years. It is now felt that, though the process must be put into motion with some care, too much puttering around with details and discussions can do more harm than good.

Greenfield vs. Redesign

Many of the more notable QWL achievements in North America have been in Greenfield sites (i.e., new plants). It is naturally more difficult to change established attitudes in an existing plant, especially where technology cannot be altered, than it is to start from scratch in an entirely new facility. Many companies that have compiled impressive records in generating innovative work organizations in new plants have been extremely reluctant to touch their older facilities. This reluctance has had a kind of reverse snowball effect, since managements in old plants have not been able to locate models to emulate. By now, however, the logjam has broken, and redesign projects have been launched in many older plants. There is perhaps a difference between Europe and the United States in this respect. In the United States, companies are free to shut down plants in one area, laying off workers, and build new plants in another. In Europe, even though one shutdown might not be related to another new construction, companies are under considerable pressure, and often specific legal requirements, to offer continuity of employment. An important factor here is the more centralized nature of European unions, compared with the stronger local autonomy that is common in U.S. unions.

The Tavistock Institute:
An Origin of Theory and Practice in QWL

There have been some notable shifts in methodologies over the past decade. Ten years ago the job enrichment approach of the U.S. psychologist Frederick Herzberg was the best-known method of creating broader and more interesting jobs, partly because it was believed to produce quick results and partly because it could be applied to individual jobs without considering other aspects of the organization or management's role. Though job enrichment did generate satisfactory results in some cases, and Herzberg's research contribution (in the 1950s) was of genuine value, job enrichment is now of much less consequence. Many independent observers recognized some years ago that it was too limited to be of great value, that its ease of application was deceptive, and that more far-reaching types of actions were needed.

By now, the dominant position has been taken over by the theories developed at the Tavistock Institute of Human Relations in London by Eric Trist, Fred Emery, A. K. Rice, Hans van Beinum, and their colleagues. The key element was the view of an organization as an open system — a sociotechnical system — encompassing not only the structure of jobs, the people doing them, and the technology, but also the interactions between these and other factors such as contiguous parts of the organization, supervision, and management roles. The theories had been developed primarily in work in the British coal mines in the 1950s and were applied on the operating level in a group of Norweigian companies in the 1960s. These Tavistock ideas have given rise to a more advanced, more sophisticated attack on the problems of work. A few U.S. behavioral scientists, principally Louis Davis of the University of California at Los Angeles, helped to diffuse these ideas among their colleagues and students. Most of the presentations at the Toronto conference were either directly representative of the Tavistock theories or heavily influenced by them.

In the past few years, some researchers have made efforts to embody some of the principal conclusions of the Tavistock theories in standardized solutions or models that then can be applied in a wide variety of situations. This, in fact, was one of the central principles in the German humanization of work programs begun in 1974, since the government felt it could not justify the heavy investment in projects custom tailored for the needs of a single site. Philips Lamp in the Netherlands also attempted to work out a set of models of production systems that could be put into operations with minor modifications in different production settings. Such efforts have produced some successes, and in many situations engineers engaged in designing a production system are able to start on a more advanced level than was the case a few years ago, and thus avoid some of the unnecessary errors of traditional engineering design. The achievements in this area have been fewer and less comprehensive than might have been hoped for, and relatively little attention has been paid to this type of development work.

Another area that has attracted little attention has been the question of costs. This is in great part because QWL specialists insist that, since each new system must be custom fitted to its environment, no predictions can be made. However, on closer examination many of the innovations worked out by QWL specialists turn out to display rather close similarities, and many of the resulting systems would lend themselves to some sort of cost-benefit analysis, particularly where innovative engineering design is a large part of the system.

An extremely strong trend, much in evidence at the Toronto conference, is the increasing number of people who, having been introduced to the potentials for improvement in their work organizations, quickly recognize the appeal of the ideas. Irwin Hopson, an operator and union secretary in the Rohm & Haas plant in Knoxville, Tennessee, had this reaction when he was first exposed to the principles of QWL: "It seemed like a great amount of information to absorb in a short time. However, we were surprised to learn that a lot of things the consultant was trying to get across to us were things we had felt all along" (Foster 1981).

FORCES BEHIND THE TRENDS

Why has QWL, which is a blend of ideas and methodologies known (at least by specialists) more than a decade ago, recently come to occupy a place of prominence in the business world? No doubt one driving force has been the perception of ever-widening circles of managers that workers, particularly younger workers, are decreasingly enthused by conventional jobs in traditional hierarchical structures. One participant at the Toronto conference — a line manager in an oil refinery — explained that he had been assigned to study probable developments in labor relations over the coming decade and saw some worrying features in the picture, "I think that if we don't do something about the way work is organized, we're going to have trouble down the road."

Though a heightened consciousness of this fact is doubtless heartening to many social thinkers who have been making this same point to anyone willing to listen throughout the 1970s, it is possible that an even stronger motivating force comes from quite a different quarter. Einar Thorsrud of the Norwegian Work Research Institute, whose pioneering work in Norwegian companies in the late 1960s helped set the stage for much of the progress that has occurred since, notes that a new and different influence is at work:

> More companies have become interested in QWL over the past few years than I would have predicted — not as many as I would like, but nevertheless more than I would have thought possible. However, the emphasis has changed from the social values inherent in QWL to productivity, and that is largely due to the influence of the Japanese and the quality circles. The idea of quality circles is having a very healthy effect. [Thorsrud, Einar, 1981]

The Change in Social Values
And the Growth of Japanese Competition

Seeing their markets being eroded by the Japanese, managers, particularly U.S. managers, have been forced to conclude that a key element in the Japanese success has been effective work organization. A number of companies, perhaps most notably Ford and General Motors, have been aggressively creating quality circles and similar organizational devices in factories to put to work the thinking power of workers in improving productivity. Thorsrud notes:

> This has a strong, cumulative effect. If General Motors is known to be doing something, other companies feel the pressure to follow. If companies use the quality circles as a quick gimmick, they won't work, and if they see that they require a considerable shift in cultural values, they will find it's not as easy as it looks. In any case, if a company tries to start quality circles and doesn't succeed, it is, in the present climate of awareness, less likely to junk the whole idea than to ask itself what mistakes it is making. This is the most important part of the trend — that companies trying and failing will not just discard the whole idea, as they might have done in the past,

but will have to ask themselves what they are doing wrong. [Thorsrud, Einar 1981]

An often overlooked dimension in this complex of factors is the pressure of competition and resulting need for flexibility, which can best be handled through solutions that are efficient from a technical point of view and at the same time improve the quality of work. For example, machine-paced assembly lines are known to be defective because they generate stress, boredom, alienation, psychologically damaging social isolation, and a generally poor work environment. But it is less widely recognized that they are inadequate in view of the urgent need in today's business environment for more flexibility and capacity to adapt to model variations and rapid shifts in product lines. A conventional assembly line cannot cope with this type of need, but small, self-regulating, multi-skilled groups can. Even if the principal motivating factor is the technical flexibility of the system, such a design might not be feasible if research by behavioral scientists had not shown that the Tayloristic model of human nature is defective and that many workers not only can cope with more demanding jobs involved in a flexible system, but prefer them. There are numerous situations such as the one just mentioned, where business pressures match the social pressures, leading to solutions that are advantageous and economical from all points of view. Indeed, many of the principles of Taylorized production systems are suboptimal, whatever the inclinations of the workers. But the more technical points are often overlooked in QWL discussions that place the emphasis on human values alone.

Despite the rising importance of productivity, the conviction remains strong among many experts that improving the quality of work is primarily a vital social necessity. Delmar Landen (1981), head of organizational development at General Motors, says: "We are dealing with a cultural revolution. . . . How long do you think we can have a free and democratic society if we insist on maintaining totalitarian systems in our companies? We must have freedom for individuals and organizations to grow and to realize their potentials."

Many managers object to the introduction of this type of social value judgment, which they see as unsuitably ideological, into the business world. Furthermore, managers are often temperamentally incompatible with behavioral scientists, whom they regard as excessively theoretical, and are skeptical of claims that improvements in efficiency and productivity can or should start with the psychological and social aspects of production systems. Behavioral scientists are sometimes unable to articulate their viewpoints in terms that managers find meaningful and on the whole have not sufficiently penetrated the intricacies of the business world to coordinate their thinking with that of managers who tend to be concerned with short-term, dollars-and-cents considerations.

Many behavioral scientists are also critical of the overly evangelical approach of some of their colleagues. Lisl Klein (1981) of the Tavistock Institute and a well-known consultant, observes:

> I am troubled by these flights into the stratosphere and talk of new worlds to conquer. We are eager to discover new concepts, but we haven't done very much to operationalize the old ones. I'd like to hear less about trust and values and other religious states of mind, and more about getting down to business.

One expert from the United Kingdom at the Toronto conference observed, "There are the people on 'Cloud Nine' living in the abstract, and then there are those who are living in the real world—and the two groups don't communicate very easily."

Most informed observers would agree that there is no crippling contradiction between behavioral science and a business orientation. Most behavioral scientists strive to include an improvement in productivity as a prime objective along with their efforts to improve the quality of working life, and there is a vast amount of solid evidence to attest to their success. But they do not always make this point sufficiently clear in their discussions. There need not be any conflict between the two groups, but there is and it has been responsible for a substantial amount of confusion in organizations. The gap between the two viewpoints is narrowing, but it would be unwise to minimize its importance.

EUROPE VS. NORTH AMERICA: CYCLES OF PROGRESS

There is no particular rivalry between Europe and North America, but their evolution has been somewhat different and these differences, which continue to influence thinking, illuminate some of the inner workings of the QWL field.

At the beginning of the 1970s, the quality of working life came into prominence quite suddenly, partly as a result of the radical spirit of the time—in Europe manifested in the French worker-student revolt in 1968, the Italian "hot autumn" of 1969, and general leftist tendencies in numerous countries; in the United States by the strike at the GM Lordstown plant in 1971 and other evidence of the "blue collar blues." At that time the best-known approach to understanding the problem was, as noted earlier, the job enrichment theory of Frederick Herzberg. The writings of other North American theorists, such as Chris Argyris, Rensis Likert, Abraham Maslow, and Douglas McGregor were also well known. Most North American companies interested in reshaping work for more satisfying jobs and better results were using the theories of these experts. While QWL activities were taking place in Europe—limited at that time to Scandinavia and the Netherlands—it was the North American experience that seemed most relevant.

During the 1970s circumstances changed in North America. Economic troubles mounted. There was a thorough deradicalization of the climate. Lordstown proved to be, not the first of a string of spontaneous revolts against the assembly line, as some observers had expected, but the first and last in the series. Monotony and boredom on the job, which for a short time was a lively topic, faded from public debate. The quality of working life seemed a low priority issue, and many companies that had been active in the field put on the brakes. At least one U.S. company that had achieved unusually good results in improving the quality of work as well as productivity virtually liquidated its effort when chill winds began to blow through the economy. In another firm, a plant that had been built as one of the most innovative new manufacturing units from an organizational point of view became a subject of bitter internal corporate dispute, and the ideas contained in the design made little impact elsewhere in the company. In some companies, where reorganization projects had begun when job enrichment was a hot topic, applications of QWL were amateurish and the results unimpressive, and projects were downgraded or completely dropped. A good many companies continued to work on the quality of work, but there was not a great push in this direction, and the level of interest among the general public sank sharply.

Increasingly in the 1970s QWL specialists both in Europe and North America adopted the Tavistock approaches. But in North America, there was so little response from some of the people who might have been expected to express an interest in the subject—line managers, engineers, government agencies, and unions—that the behavioral scientists interested in the Tavistock ideas were talking primarily to other behavioral scientists. A consequence of this was that thinking stagnated to some extent from lack of active discussion. If the theories had been knocked about a bit in debate among the interested parties, there might have been a more vigorous development of the intellectual climate. This has resulted in a certain aridity in the theories and approaches of the North American specialists, which is still to some extent apparent.

European Development and Diffusion of QWL in the 1970s

In Europe, there had been a similar flare-up of interest in QWL among the general public at the beginning of the 1970s, and a similar decline. But there were critical differences. Considerable impetus to develop new approaches came from a number of sources, which varied from country to country — governments (either specialized agencies established for this purpose or politicians recognizing an issue with potential appeal to certain groups), employers' associations (extremely powerful, semigovernmental bodies that have no counterparts in North America), unions, and a more leftist political climate than existed in North America.

There was considerable discussion, and some legislation, on several drastically different facets of the quality of working life, for example, requirements that companies place worker representatives on boards of directors and heavy worker involvement in safety and health and other internal company matters. Perhaps becuase so many conflicting forces were at work and so many disparate objectives had to be taken into consideration, a highly fragmented and unsystematic patchwork of approaches and theories resulted.

The Tavistock ideas played a dominant role in Europe as in North America, but there were many detours, deviations, and variations on the Tavistock themes. In North America, the Tavistock ideas were diffused by a relatively small number of experts — behavioral scientists, or persons oriented to the behavioral sciences — who relayed their ideas primarily to other experts with similar orientations. In Europe, ideas on QWL were spread by and among more different types of people — arguably a more cumbersome and bureaucratic process, but one enriched by inputs from numerous quarters and generating a body of knowledge with more facets and nuances than was the case in North America — and consequently much more varied, and perhaps also closer to reality. This was less true of Canada than of the United States, inasmuch as Canadian government bodies (both federal and provincial) and unions took a more active and aggressive interest in QWL, than did their counterparts in the United States. In this respect, Canada is closer to Europe than to the United States.

Some examples of the diffusion process in Europe can be instructive. In Sweden the QWL field was to a great extent taken over by SAF, the Swedish Employers' Confederation, which meant that approaches recommended to companies reflected the preoccupations of line managers and engineers. Although the SAF methods were heavily influenced by behavioral scientists' conclusions, the methodologies incorporated large measures of industrial engineering and productivity improvement. This has not been altogether to the liking of unions and their supporters (who would have preferred more emphasis on legislated systems of participation) and some other researchers (who would have liked more dominance by behavioral scientists).

In Germany there are relatively small numbers of behavioral scientists, and many of those who are active are believed to adopt exaggeratedly leftist positions and are thus regarded with much suspicion by managers. In addition, the rigid legislation regarding works councils makes it difficult to obtain participation of employees in designing their own organizations or to use semiautonomous groups. The unions, especially the powerful metal-workers' union, are constantly on guard to ensure that infringements of their authority do not occur. This situation fits in with the German humanization of work projects where the emphasis is on engineering design of systems that can be widely applied in various production systems without sounding out employee reactions. It is therefore engineers, rather than behavioral scientists, who dominate the projects. The findings of behavioral science receive a considerable amount of attention (Lisl Klein of the Tavistock Institute has been serving as a consultant to the German government on this subject for a number of years), but they are applied in system design by engineers.

In Italy the initiative was seized at an early stage by the unions, which pressured large companies to improve jobs at the same time they were putting forth other demands, and specific measures for improving the quality of working life were frequently written into contracts. (For example, this is the reason Fiat organized production around "islands" instead of a line at one plant, and its Cassino plant was located at Cassino in response to a union demand that the company invest in the economically depressed Mezzogiorno.) When managements took the initiative, the unions insisted on the right to monitor closely and to comanage. In all cases the unions have watched carefully to see that workers' interests were being promoted. On the other hand, they have generally refused to take any interest in productivity, which they have maintained is the company's problem not theirs. The rejection of union responsibility for productivity may have been tactically unwise; when the economic crisis arrived, the unions were forced to de-emphasize QWL and to concentrate their energies on bread-and-butter issues such as the reduction of unemployment.

Governments have developed a keen interest in QWL. State agencies promote QWL in the United Kingdom, France, Belgium, Germany, and the Netherlands, and various conflicting viewpoints have to be integrated in the agencies' activities. In Norway, legislation requires companies to design production systems in accordance with principles of participative management. The consequence of this friction with diverse and sometimes alien forces in many European countries is that the QWL theories invented by behavioral scientists have integrated a wider range of objectives into their operational structure than is the case in North America.

During the recent past, it may fairly be said that there has been an explosion of interest in QWL in North America in the form of a sharper focus on events that were taking place a bit out of the limelight during the 1970s and a new burst of activity in places where QWL had been dormant or nonexistent for some time. As noted earlier, this new wave of activity has been in great part because of the fascination with Japanese quality circles. It should be noted that these quality circles do not involve appreciable changes in jobs but are concentrated primarily on creating positive worker attitudes. Some of the U.S. effort has been directed toward copying the Japanese, which fits in well with the preexisting orientation of QWL experts toward the psychological and social aspects of work. General Motors, for example, has established great numbers of quality circles, but little change has occurred in the GM Assembly Division, which is noted for having devised some of the most highly Taylorized and objectionable jobs in the company.

There has been no comparable explosion of QWL activity in Europe — perhaps because the Japanese invasion there has been less aggressive than in North America, or perhaps for other reasons. Progress in QWL is being made at a steady pace, but in terms of practical applications the position of leadership (if there is one) now seems to be in North America.

One Swede at the Toronto conference gave this impression of the differences between Europe and North America at the present time, "The Europeans are using more complicated and more sophisticated techniques than the Americans — but the Americans are doing much more than the Europeans." Some Europeans, however, find that North American QWL efforts are dominated by vacuous discussions of principles and idealistic theorizing by behavioral scientists. According to Karl Furmaniak, project manager of the German humanization of work program: "You have the rhetoric — we have more of the reality of QWL."

QWL IN CORPORATE STRATEGY

The Policy of AT&T

While the improvement of QWL has become a top priority item in a number of large and small companies, the nature of the strategy employed in its implementation varies considerably. At American Telephone and Telegraph, QWL has become a concern of top management, and in 1980 notice was sent to all the operating companies in the Bell System on the implementation of this new element in the company's policy.

In addition, QWL objectives were integrated in the contract with the Communications Workers of America (CWA) in 1980. Ronnie Straw (1981) of the CWA says: "We thought the QWL part of the contract was the most important."

One factor behind these developments was a slowly growing lack of trust between management and workers. Surveys of employee attitudes showed that workers felt management did not trust them. Moreover, they believed that computer systems were robbing them of some of the autonomy they prized in their jobs. A worker participation program had been started, but it was seen as a one-way street by the employees. They did not feel their ideas were taken seriously — the objectives were only productivity improvement, not the employees' experience of their work. To the unions, this signaled the dangers of unilateral management control.

The CWA contacted Michael Maccoby, the noted psychiatrist, social thinker, and consultant, who concluded that union involvement in the participation system would bring about a significant change. This could benefit both the company and the union: the workers would be more cooperative if they perceived that their views were being considered, and the union could be sure that its values would be promoted and its interests protected. The objective of participation jointly agreed upon and included in the contract was "to solve the problems when they occur where they occur — by the people who have to live with the solutions." The contract also specified that there would be no layoffs or speed-ups as a result of the participation program; freedom to file grievances would not be disturbed; the unions would not object to increased productivity; the unions would be involved in all phases of the program; and an emphasis would be placed on individual dignity. A joint national committee was formed to pursue the goals with Maccoby as consultant.

From the union's point of view, the most serious problem is management. The CWA's Straw (1981) says that, "they want to present finished projects to the union for approval, while in many areas the union is bogged down in cosmetic arrangements. If that's the limit of participation, then it's no good."

The management side concedes that it has a lot to learn. In the words of Lilian Lynch (1981) of Illinois Bell (where the process of applying the contract has gone further than in most other units): "You can't just talk about QWL — you have to live it. Training in QWL is absolutely necessary. I hadn't thought so at first, but you have to unlearn what you thought you knew and then learn all over again."

The process is still in its early stages, but both sides are optimistic. Straw says, "We believe worker participation will have a major impact on the company."

QWL and General Motors

General Motors has been somewhat concerned with QWL for a number of years and has quite recently launched a major drive to improve the quality of working life in its plants. Its recent interest is a result of the Japanese competition, which is suspected of being strongly propelled by the quality circles, and research into the concrete effects of worker discontent. GM's Delmar Landen notes:

The correlation between absenteeism increases above 8 percent and increasing in-process defects .93—almost a perfect correlation. You add more inspection, which generates more defects, since workers subconsciously feel less pressure, and this leads to more repairs and more overtime.

The basis of the GM program is the creation of new organizational structures and interrelationships that rule the activities of the people. Landen says:

If we are sincere about making QWL more than a passive social science blip on the industrial screen, so to speak, we are going to have to create organizational systems that institutionalize the norms, the boundaries, and the cultures which are the elements of the QWL process. Delegation, shifting of responsibilities, new configurations of decision making—these things are not going to happen if we do not create the organizational structures, the empowering mechanisms that give people the knowledge and skills they need for responsible decision making.

The objective is thus to establish these new structures at every level of the organization, train people to become more involved in decision making, and then let them move into the new structural mechanism. GM is working hard to refine and improve this process. Landen says that a problem at the Tarrytown plant—site of a heavily publicized participation program that began to unravel when personnel changes were made in the plant management—was that training was not followed through with the creation of a structural mechanism in which the training could be used. At other plants, such as Fisher Body Detroit, a similar program was put into operation, but those coming out of the training who wished to could move immediately into an employee participation group—a "structural participative mechanism."

Most of the GM work has been on organizational structures and relations between people—not on technology. The General Motors Assembly Division, which has acquired a reputation for creating some of the most objectionable jobs in GM, continues to operate much in its traditional pattern.

QWL and Alcoa

The Aluminum Corporation of America has a considerably different approach. In 1972 the company built its first plant, in Ohio, based on the Tavistock open system approach similar to that used so successfully by Procter and Gamble (P&G), and using the same consultants as those employed by P&G. It was organized around groups and was a unionized operation (United Automobile Workers [UAW]). In the mid-1970s another new plant was built in Texas, also unionized (United Steelworkers [USW]), in which the QWL aspects were covered in the contract, which has since been renewed twice with this part essentially intact. In the 1980 national USW contract, QWL was again a feature. Perhaps more significant for the future than this series of separate projects is an overall policy plan that was drawn up over a period of a year by a special committee. The committee visited 70 other companies and made recommendations of technological and organizational design, human resources planning and development, and productivity. The committee's recommendations were sent to all officers of the company, and those that were approved were included in the Advanced Management Program.

David Mader, productivity director at Alcoa, explains that this program is designed to guide the company's development in the 1980s: "We're going to crank this into all sites in the company. Managers will have the opportunity to develop their own plans. They will have a considerable amount of autonomy. But they will have to have a plan."

The program includes a number of principles that are intended to replace the previously accepted conventional wisdom. Some examples of the new principles follow:

New Principles	Traditional Principles
Utilize the thinking of every employee who can improve organization effectiveness.	"Workers work and managers think."
Management perceives its power to be earned through leadership and know-how.	Management perceives its power to come from prerogatives and level of position.
Both human asset management and financial performance management are measured and rewarded or penalized accordingly.	Human asset management subservient to financial performance management.
Job design balances people needs with technology needs.	Lowest common denominator job design for maximum control.
Worker rewards meet self-esteem and societal needs.	Worker rewards are predominantly wage, benefit, and security oriented.

QWL and General Foods

A different type of evolution has been demonstrated in the case of General Foods (GF). The famous GF plant at Topeka, Kansas, was completed in 1971. This plant was, and still is, regarded as an outstanding example of modern production systems design, incorporating group operation, broadened jobs, high skills levels, a low level of supervision, and heavy employee involvement in plant management matters. The plant has attracted considerable attention, both in North America and abroad, and a similar GF plant located in Rheims, France, was completed a couple of years later. Job satisfaction was high and unit costs were extraordinarily low. This writer happened to visit both of these plants shortly after they were put on stream. Both were impressive in their use of unconventional production systems — with complex work patterns built into the engineering design — and participative supervisory practices. The French version was less advanced than the Topeka plant, but compared with customary authoritarian French management practices, it was remarkable in terms of job satisfaction as well as productivity.

In recent years, much controversy has swirled around the Topeka plant. Since its earliest days, it has aroused suspicion and hostility within General Foods among managers who could not accept the unorthodox practices. Various reports circulated that the original ideas were fading under the conformist pressures from corporate headquarters, which had been chipping away at some unique features of the Topeka system. This seemed to be confirmed by the departure from GF of some of the managers who had been identified with the plant's design and operation. The most perplexing aspect of the situation was the failure of the Topeka innovations to be copied on any appreciable scale elsewhere in GF.

In Toronto, a team of employees from Topeka, including the plant manager, made a presentation of the "ten year young" history of the plant, the first time in many years that any extensive information has come from GF. The group explained that some changes had taken place in the plant over the years. Many of them were more or less ordinary adaptations (decided upon by the employees) in the face of routine problems, such as resolution of some friction in the functioning of plant work teams through a merger of teams that made it easier for employees to shift between jobs. A more troublesome event was the introduction of a new procedure for hiring — replacement of a team-managed process by a more carefully codified, bureaucratic set of steps. This change was prompted by fears of violating the Equal Employment Opportunity Act, but it caused some resentment among employees because they were neither consulted nor adequately informed of the reasons for the change — a slip-up that management now concedes was an error. The group also gave hints of some struggles with corporate headquarters, such as an attempt to replace the employee-managed plant purchasing procedure with appointment of a conventional purchasing manager. The plant countered with a proposal to retain something of its own system but slightly more formalized and with better control; the plant won this argument. The group declined to comment on questions regarding the reports of hostility within the corporation to the Topeka concept. Herm Simon, the plant manager, noted that "sometimes we get our way and sometimes we don't, but we have a fairly good batting average." He emphasized that such disagreement was normal in any company.

In any case, it seems that the essential elements of the plant are still in operation, even though outsiders might conclude that being on the defensive is scarcely conducive to further development of the participative system. The group spoke with considerable pride of the plant's unusual system, the respected position it enjoys in its community (more than 1,000 unsolicited job applications are received each year, more than three times the number of employees), and its continuing favorable operating figures (low costs, high quality, and productivity improvements in nine of the ten years since the plant was completed).

Volvo: A Position of Prominence

Doubtless the most innovative European company in matters of work organization is Volvo, the Swedish car and truck manufacturer. The company has attained this position in part due to the strong views on the organization of work held by its president, Pehr Gyllenhammar, and, in part due to the social and labor legislation in Sweden, which alleviates the penalties on workers who stay off the job at the same time it applies pressure on companies to improve work environments and working conditions. Expectations that the company would take the lead in this field would in any case be automatically high since it is Sweden's largest manufacturing company and is an industry in which the proportion of rotten jobs has traditionally been large.

The company's campaign to improve jobs began in the 1960s, partly as a result of the company's experiences with works councils (management-worker joint consultation bodies, established in Sweden in the early post-war period), and partly because of experiments, initiated at various sites by supervisors, engineers, union representatives or workers, in job rotation, autonomous group operation, and other relatively mild forms of work reorganization, often motivated by ergonomic considerations.

In 1971–72, the company moved out of this stage of "disconnected trials" and into a new and more aggressive developmental stage, building on the experience gained in the earlier work. Berth Jönsson (1981), Volvo's corporate planning director, says:

> No company can afford to continue experimenting on this broad scale. It must create a strategy and decide how to go about implementing it in the most efficient manner. We are right now in an advanced stage of the second

phase which includes new creative solutions to flexible hardware technology and the diffusion of ideas in Volvo subsidiaries outside of Sweden.

One of the earliest, and still the most famous, results of the strategic planning was the novel final assembly plant at Kalmar, completed in 1974, where the conventional straight line machine-paced assembly line, with short-cycle jobs excluding use of operators' initiative, was replaced by a series of production islands separated by buffers based on the work of multi-skilled, self-regulating groups.

This plant became, for rather irrelevant reasons, highly controversial, and for a time was discussed outside Sweden as a failure that would never be repeated. This was not the case, and nine Volvo plants finished since that time have incorporated some of the Kalmar ideas. They have also used features in the next generation of technology after Kalmar. For example, in the Kalmar plant car bodies move through the assembly operation on sleek, noiseless trolleys following magnetic tracks embedded in the floor. Some later plants go a step further — units under assembly are transported on hovercraftlike cushions of air.

There are a number of levels of job improvement at Volvo. In the first step, the cycle is lengthened and the number of separate tasks is increased (horizontal job enlargement). On a second level of complexity, jobs are expanded vertically, to include such items as inspection of incoming materials, materials handling, quality control, adjustment for defects, tooling and retooling, and maintenance. At the third level, groups of operators participate in production planning, rationalization projects, hiring procedures, evaluating output, and technical development (tools, and so forth). So far, this third level has received only limited application.

Obviously progression from the first of these levels through the others increasingly involves organizational change rather than the reshaping of individual jobs. Two programs that serve as support systems are a series of lectures and discussions about products, and various courses in interpersonal relations, group working and problem solving.

At Volvo the effort to improve the quality of working life is a high priority, comprehensive company-wide project. For Gyllenhammar, Volvo's president, this is a most urgent and serious matter: "The working man needs a sense of purpose and satisfaction in his daily work. He feels the need of belonging to a team, of being able to identify himself with the goods he produces and — not least — of feeling that he is appreciated for the work he performs" (Jönsson 1981). So strong are Gyllenhammar's convictions on this subject that he may be said to have imposed democratic organizational forms in an authoritarian manner. The unconventional Volvo design evolved from a Gyllenhammar dictate regarding the general principles to be incorporated.

He rejected some preliminary insufficiently daring proposals, after which the engineers were sent back to the drawing board to try again.

One of the lessons the company has learned in its efforts on QWL, according to Jönsson, is that, even though a positive management attitude to change is essential, if this turns into an overly rigid "endeavor to impose programs projects and plans 'from above' we tend to fail." The company also feels that, for best results, "initiatives for change must come from the 'line' and not from white collar specialists." Moreover, it is advisable to regard organizational innovations as being without fixed limits — over time and through the organization. "Changes in the work situation must include a 'package' of activities introduced over a period of time. . . . Isolated trials with the introduction of, for instance, simple job rotation, are doomed to failure" (Jönsson 1981).

Sherex Chemical:
The Early Stages of Implementation

Some instructive insights into current QWL practices can be gained by looking at companies still in their early stages of entering the field. At the Mapleton, Illinois, plant of Sherex Chemical, management saw a number of reasons for launching a QWL project. First, there was a history of poor labor relations, including one lengthy strike, costly for both sides. Kenneth Johnson, the plant manager, explains that, "After this, I was convinced there must be a better way." Boredom was a problem. Management felt that the traditional supervisory job had to be changed if the supervisors were going to stay on the job, but it was not possible to redesign their jobs without also changing the operators' jobs. Of the latter, Johnson says:

> The company and the union had cooperated in creating boring jobs, easy to learn, with no challenge. We got highly qualified applicants but never asked for their ideas, suggestions, or participation in decision making. We had good workers but didn't use these valuable assets.

In late 1979 the plant hired Lyman Ketchum, the consultant, to help start a QWL project. It was decided that the plant would be suitable for a QWL project based on sociotechnical analysis. Ketchum discussed the project with plant management, with workers, and with the company president. A steering group was composed, consisting of the plant manager and his staff, the union executive committee, and one first line supervisor. A core group, a unit of about 35 people where bad attendance, productivity difficulties, and an undisciplined work force were some of the headaches, was picked to start. Some of the problems encountered in the early stages were: middle managers felt left out of the proceedings; there seemed no way to measure success; foremen felt threatened by job insecurity; and QWL was often viewed as a short-term experiment. The rejection of QWL by managers presented a problem that had to be handled with training. The company quickly gave employees a no-layoff guarantee and assurance that decertification was not a goal.

The program has been in operation a little over a year and has not produced any concrete results, though both managers and the union feel that personal relationships are better. Bob Morrison, a supervisor, who notes that the supervisors thought the project would never work and that employees would never be able to participate usefully in plant management matters, has modified his position somewhat: "I was assigned to the core group. We decided to follow all the steps in manufacturing one of our products. In doing this, we found several problems in some operations. We discussed them and found some solutions. That showed us that this technical analysis had some merit."

Rohm & Haas:
QWL and the Need to Introduce
a New System of Work

The Knoxville, Tennessee, plant of Rohm & Haas started a QWL project primarily because a major product, plexiglass, was facing some serious new competition, and the plant's survival seemed to depend on the successful introduction of an extensive computerized real-time information system and a rearranged work flow to reduce materials-handling costs.

A first phase was to be in the plexiglass finishing and shipping unit, a high volume, labor intensive operation producing 25,000 sheets per week and designed to handle 22,000 separate items. The program woud change or eliminate numerous jobs. The normal method would be to announce the plans, put them into effect immediately, and try to wear away the resistance. But there was a desire to avoid this type of confrontation this time. Joe Foster (1981), production manager, notes:

> Our studies indicated that a design around whole jobs could result in a better plant, and that the sociotechnical approach would be more effective. We also felt that the involvement of operating people, hourly employees and foremen, in the design would produce a better design and reduce resistance.

A consultant was hired and a pilot project developed in loose sheet handling. It was hoped that the pilot project could be handled by a task force of salaried and hourly employees whose objectives would be to improve customer service, increase the return on investment, and create a good working environment (the first time the latter had ever been established as a goal in such a process). The situation and the idea were revealed to union representatives in an unprecedented presentation, noting that jobs would be eliminated, but offering a no-layoff commitment in return for union cooperation. After some lengthy skirmishing, the union accepted, and the task force was set up with representation of the union, management, and employees, plus the consultant.

The task force began with presentations by the union and management sides of their understandings of the QWL process. There was some trouble connecting the social and technical aspects, but management focused on the technical, and the union side on the social, which on the whole appeared to be a good arrangement. The task force development period proved, according to a union member, to be a time of "learning, growth, testing, crises, frustration and evolution of trust between the members." There were some considerable strains, but after eight months of work the group presented a concrete set of proposals, which involved considerable change in layout and would reduce operations in the pilot area from ten moves and seven storages to three moves and two storages, eliminate three employees, cut worker classifications involved from six job grades to three, and the department boundaries from six to three. The proposal included data on payback time of investment, return on gross assets, discounted cash flow, and adverse conditions that might affect the design. Irwin Hopson, a union member, says: "The redesign, so I'm told, is radical enough to compare with any design ever done at a greenfield site."

According to management the proposal, which was accepted after some "crises in trust with that group" due to a need to modify it, was attractive because it would reduce dependence on other departments in producing plexiglass mirrors. A year after the task force had begun its work, training of operators for the new self-regulating team operation began, with a temporary new arrangement of equipment (prior to final engineering changes). After five more months, the process of turning over the operation to the team began. The operators now schedule production, arrange for all mechanical work, order and maintain supplies, and negotiate with the raw materials supplier. About 15 people had been trained for the new teams, and about 10 members of self-regulating teams are in development. Altogether, about 150 people (25 percent of the plant's work force) have been involved in the program.

From the company's point of view, the object of the exercise is greater efficiency. Joe Mettalia (1981), the area manager for plexiglass mirrors, says:

> We haven't yet seen a bottom line improvement in productivity, but I'm
> convinced that, if it comes, it will be because our people are on board and
> involved rather than because we have contrived some technical improve-

ments. We've learned that, if you set up a group to devise a new work structure, you must have a continuing dialogue between that group and operating personnel. All the potentially involved supervisory personnel and line personnel need significant training and practice in the new participative management mode. The turnover of supervisory work responsibilities to operators needs to be done as soon as possible. Worker involvement only becomes significant when the workers can actually see the supervisors stepping back and allowing them to control. We think we have a higher degree of trust, but we must continue to build on this base.

QWL IMPACT ON UNIONS

Labor unions have been in an ambivalent position regarding efforts to improve the organization of work—torn between a desire to get better working conditions for their members (which QWL does) and a reluctance to encourage workers to identify with management goals (which QWL also tends to do). The suspicion that QWL may reduce union loyalties is based on facts. Some well-known innovations in work organization have been put through in nonunion settings where employees became so satisfied with their work that they are unusually indifferent to union organizing attempts. One management consultant, formerly a personnel officer of a large U.S. company, has openly promoted his services in improving the quality of working life as a means of combating unions.

In the past, both unions and companies were caught badly off balance by the new challenge of QWL. The unions were undoubtedly remiss in not recognizing how they could use QWL in helping their members—and how companies could use it against them. Many of the pioneering QWL projects were in nonunion plants, but often this was because managements did not know, and did not take the trouble to examine, the potential fit between the new QWL ideas and union policies.

By now, however, numerous union leaders have become acquainted with QWL, and there were some 250 unionists at the Toronto conference. In many cases presentations of company case histories were made jointly by managers and union officials, which would have been inconceivable only a few years ago. The reasons for union interest in QWL are, in part, the same as those offered by managers; jobs that contain more responsibility, and thus are more satisfying, are also frequently more productive. Irving Bluestone (1981), former vice president of the United Automobile Workers, remarks that: "Workers want to perform their jobs well; they want to produce a quality product. . . . They recognize that good quality is tied inevitably to improved job security through assured sales."

Bluestone was, around 1970, the first top labor official in North America to develop an interest in QWL. By a happy coincidence, this interest proved of great value when the U.S. auto companies began using worker participation to improve quality and productivity. The UAW now acts as a partner and, in a sense, comanager of the participative management programs in force at Ford and GM. Chrysler's appointment of a UAW official on its board of directors in return for union help in meeting the company's financial crisis is participation of a different sort, but is nevertheless recognition of workers' capacity to carry more responsibility than they have had the chance to do in the past.

Another notable example of union involvement is the steel industry, also suffering from foreign competition, where the United Steelworkers has entered into agreements on far-reaching participation in management matters. Sam Camens (1981), an official of the United Steelworkers, states that one of the underlying reasons for the industry's troubles was an overly authoritarian management style that had a heavy influence on the reaction of workers: "When they came into a plant they came into a totally autocratic world; alienation is scarcely the word for it—it was more like total hatred for the whole system." Camens is optimistic about the potentials of the 1980 contract provision on worker participation, which he feels "may turn out to be more important than anything else in the contract." Some other North American unions that are actively cooperating in QWL projects include the Communication Workers of America, the Oil, Chemical and Atomic Workers, and the United Glass and Ceramic Workers. Representatives of all these were at the Toronto conference.

Confrontation and Collaboration

Even though QWL activities serve to reduce unnecessary and unproductive labor-management friction, few managers see any possibility that it will basically alter the union's adversarial role. David Mader (1981) of Alcoa points out: "Some managers have asked how we are going to eliminate adversarial relationships. We are not going to eliminate them. We feel that union relationships will inevitably be alternately adversarial and collaborative, and we are only trying to increase the collaborative element." Art Kube (1981), an official of the Canadian Labour Congress, agrees that a high level of strife is not essential: "After all, the unions are not interested in having constant confrontation policies. It does not fulfill any useful purpose."

The unions are frequently finding that it is poor tactics to stay out of QWL activities. At Sherex Chemical, the union withdrew its participation from the QWL project in retaliation for a company dismissal of an employee—but came back six weeks later. A union official explained, "we felt we had too much to lose by not participating in QWL." At the Rohm & Haas Knoxville, Tennessee plant, the union considered, then rejected, an offer by management to participate in a QWL project. After six months during which management went it alone, the union voted to change its mind because, as the union president said, "maybe we shouldn't refuse something we knew nothing about."

Some Gains for Unions' Involvement in QWL

The union role in QWL is commonly discussed in terms of risks and potential negative impacts on union goals. Usually overlooked are the ways a union may benefit, but here are some, cited by Edward Cohen-Rosenthal (1981), a U.S. consultant: access to information, avoidance of management mistakes, better public relations, more money to bargain over, increased support for union leadership, improved health and safety, reduced stress, less unnecessary supervision, and improved interpersonal relations.

Where unions have been involved in QWL projects, it has been customary for the involvement to be formalized in a written agreement establishing a joint labor-management steering group, containing job security and seniority rights, and generally sketching out the objectives of the project. In some cases, the cooperation is discussed in the normal collective bargaining process and included in the contract.

In North America even though the unions have often demanded and received various types of protection of their interests, their participation tends to be passive—limited to watching management-initiated activities and ensuring that the promised benefits to workers actually accrue. So far North American unions have not made any more aggressive demands in connection with the organization of work, though other approaches are possible as has been shown in Europe.

One of the best-known examples of union involvement in such matters was seen in Germany, in the 1973 strike by the metalworking union in Nordbaden-Nordwurttemberg. After a two-week strike, the union won a 55-point package of "humanization of work" measures, ranging from protection for older workers to establishment of a minimum 90-minute task cycle on new, machine-paced assembly lines. The contract led to concrete improvements in working environments in some factories and, perhaps more importantly, sensitized other unions as well as managers to the importance of "humanization" issues in the work environment. It also was part of the pressure for the launching of the government's humanization of work program the following year. As mentioned earlier, German legislation is interpreted by the union as barring some usual features of work reorganization projects.

Another frequent union demand is for higher wages, for example, an automatic upgrading of everyone affected by a reorganization project as an advance dividend on the higher productivity management expects. Needless to say, managements strive to resist such demands.

In Sweden the unions have objected vociferously to projects initiated and run by managements since they did not give workers sufficiently solid influence over meaningful aspects of company operations, but only over the immediate work place. These projects had often been described as "industrial democracy," but the unions maintained that this was a highly misleading label. These objections were part of the unions' campaign to win stronger rights through legislation, which they in fact did in the 1976 Codetermination Law, granting workers the right to negotiate over any aspect of company operations and in fact requiring managements to offer to negotiate on important matters before decisions are taken. Similar arguments have been started by the Dutch unions, which managed to delay a government-sponsored series of work structuring experiments for some years while they discussed a demand that the unions be fully involved and that the projects not be narrowly limited to aspects of individual jobs. The unions won this skirmish but elsewhere have frequently acted to discourage work structuring projects.

In France the unions are quite ideologically oriented and sometimes refuse to be involved in projects on the grounds that their cooperation would only serve to buttress the capitalist system. The unions are extremely weak, and only occasionally does this attitude prove genuinely troublesome. But the threat of union objections plays a definite role, and this is one reason that French companies tend to be highly secretive about their activities in improving work organization.

TECHNOLOGY AND QWL

In the nineteenth century when workers first began to combine forces to obtain more control over their work, they placed heavy emphasis on the deskilling effects of industrialization as well as on wage questions, but because employers were particularly resistant to pressure on such matters, workers' energies were gradually channeled almost exclusively into wage questions.

Today, much attention is again being directed to this issue of deskilling by advanced technology. However, there is insufficient concrete understanding of the connections between new technologies and how they can and will affect the quality of working life.

Sociotechnical Systems as a Design Concept

As mentioned earlier, one of the central concepts in the Tavistock school of thought was that of the sociotechnical system — a view of an organization as not merely a technical system, which had been the traditional approach taken by engineers, or primarily a social system, which was a tack taken by some social scientists, but a total organism in which various aspects interact. This basic idea is rather simple and the solutions are limited in number — that is, the jobs and the organization around the technology may be adapted to make a better fit with the technical system, or the technology may be adapted to fit around the social system (or what is believed to be a desirable social system), or some of both.

The first method is the approach adopted in the early experiments in the United Kingdom (U.K.) coal fields (launched because new machinery was not generating the productivity that had been calculated), which resulted in considerable boosts in productivity through allowing workers to restore some features of the old social system (Trist et al. 1963). Though this was some 30 years ago and the human problems triggered by the introduction of new technology continue to be much discussed, few of those concerned with new equipment have focused on these problems. At the Toronto conference, Oliver Tynan reported that the Work Research Unit, the U.K. government agency that he heads, sent a group to a large trade show of robots and other new types of equipment and asked every exhibitor about the consideration given to human concerns in designing the equipment — not a single exhibitor gave a positive response.

Most companies purchasing the equipment largely neglect the question as well. According to a study of computer integrated manufacturing systems by Melvin Blumberg and Donald Gerwin (1981) of the University of Wisconsin, "Too much attention has been paid to development of technology and not enough to the adjustments needed in organizations to accommodate the technology." The study showed that workers in such installations experience many of the familiar symptoms of alienation — abnormally low variety, task significance, feedback, meaningfulness of the work, and knowledge of results. The authors conclude:

> We seem to be galloping headlong into a valley of technological chaos. ... New manufacturing technology is being designed with little regard for the skills, attitudes and systems and procedures necessary to support it. Consequently, technical complexity is outstripping the capabilities of firms to deal with it. [Blumberg and Gerwin 1981]

Many companies invest in this type of equipment without the means to evaluate the cost-effectiveness either of the equipment itself or the actual operating environment in which it will function.

In the case of some rather standard types of technology that have been in use for some time, means have been found to make better use of the technology and at the same time create a more human system. One key is to avoid simply dropping an advanced piece of equipment in the place of an old piece of equipment; it is preferable to rethink the entire process, the technology as well as the jobs. Substituting a numerically controlled machine tool for a conventional machine tool, for example, can have a negative effect on a system, since the operator can no longer make adequate use of his skills, has less control over the machine, and often is more closely tied to a line operation. With retraining, however, he can do setting-up, programming, and some maintenance, meaning that the job is broader and more interesting and the overall operation is smoother and more resistant to disturbances. A study in Germany showed that where conventional numerically controlled machine tools were in operation low-skilled workers could be used, but in the case of computerized numerically controlled machine tools, the machines could be programmed on the shop floor and therefore advantageously operated by skilled workers. Skilled workers were operating the conventional numerically controlled machines in 42 percent of the cases, but the computerized numerically controlled machines in 78 percent of the cases.

A step beyond this type of somewhat passive adaptation to machines is the design of production systems with a particular social system in mind. A classic case is the above-mentioned Volvo Kalmar assembly plant, where social and psychological considerations were built into the architecture and engineering design. The building is multi-cornered, and a group of operators for an assembly stage is located in its own corner with its own locker room, shower, and entrance to enhance the group feeling. Since assembly is separated into groups, broad, relatively long-cycle jobs are part of the system, but to some extent operators may design their own jobs. A buffer system frees operators from the pace of the line.

Obviously, the functioning of the Kalmar system does not depend on the human organization or management styles alone — in fact, many features are so firmly embedded in the design that it would be impossible for an antipathetic manager to alter them.

It is perhaps because of this revolutionary aspect of the design that the plant aroused such strong antagonism in its early years. Lisl Klein says: "A successful and sustained experiment arouses a lot of resentment. There was a large increase in the flow of tourists to Sweden due to people intent on proving that the Volvo experiment doesn't work." At the Toronto conference, Berth Jönsson felt impelled to offer assurances that Kalmar was not a failure.

A somewhat similar basic concept is seen in Fiat's newly designed asynchronous engine assembly, scheduled to be in operation soon. Designed for engine assembly, this new system is built around a series of modules, each consisting of one or more bench stations, interspersed with automatic operations and connected by buffers. Maria-Theresa Schutt of Fiat notes that the "main objective is to provide generally improved working conditions by eliminating the workers' tight interdependence with the assembly line and with each other, to give individual operators a certain amount of operating flexibility."

If it is possible to design improvements in the human organization into the engineering of individual systems, then it should be possible to design improvements into components of systems that could then be combined into larger systems. Substantial amounts of such development have, in fact, been done in Germany where researchers have developed standardized models of assembly and machining line design, buffers, and configurations of production systems that combat stress in various types of jobs.

The Swedes have been developing similar organizational solutions, but concentrating on the design of entire factories or production units. A group known as the "new factories" project has been collecting, and attempting to systematize, examples of innovative Swedish factory design that offer a favorable fit of the social and technical systems. For example, it is generally accepted that the smaller the unit the more acceptable it is to the employees, but there is not a great abundance of knowledge of how this may be done in economically advantageous ways. The Swedish group has been developing methods of shrinking the size of organizations in ways that will also improve their efficiency. Many large units doing batch production can be split into small "factories within factories" to produce families of similar products. The outcomes can include more satisfying jobs, higher productivity, faster throughput times, lower in-process inventories, simpler planning processes, less supervision, and better quality. These may be offset by higher initial investment or other factors, but often the balance is nevertheless in favor of smaller units. In any case, this method of attack offers a means of assessing the costs. Similarly, assembly lines may be split into parallel "flow groups," which not only do away with the stress and monotony of short-cycle, machine-paced jobs, but are also more flexible (model variations may be easily introduced), and more resistant to disturbances (on a long assembly line, if one person is absent from his post, the entire line stops).

At the Toronto conference, Jan Edgren of the Swedish Management Group (a consulting firm affiliated with the Swedish Employers' Confederation) offered some guidelines on calculating the cost-effectiveness of such solutions. Edgren notes that this approach, which has been largely promoted by the Swedish Employers' Confederation, has attracted considerable criticism from the left in Sweden. Edgren (1981) comments: "Only principles that are economically efficient will in the long run prove themselves to be viable. It is such principles that must be the foundation upon which a better working life can be created. We simply cannot afford anything else."

QWL specialists often object to the use of "canned" designs on the grounds that a system must be designed from scratch to fit the circumstances.

Nevertheless, some basic principles and problems do not have to be re-searched from zero for each new system — such as the stress caused by short-cycle jobs, workers' dislike for machine-paced assembly lines, the prefer-ence of most workers for group working, and the greater opportunities for social satisfaction presented by smaller units. A knowledge of tested solu-tions can thus be extremely valuable. However thorough the design process for a particular system, the designers must possess a "vocabulary" of system components and the meaning of each for the total design. This is the ap-proach being taken by, most notably, the Institute for Production Technol-ogy and Automation in Stuttgart, Germany, and the Swedish Employers' Confederation.

CONCLUSION

This chapter has focused on the present status of QWL and its evolution over the past decade. What about the future?

Some observers believe that QWL may be a fad that will disappear with a changing public mood. This seems unlikely. It has been well recog-nized that there is a choice in designing organizations, and that the differ-ence between a good and bad choice may have a heavy impact on results. The probability is that this fact will become more influential, not less. To be sure, the subject will unquestionably continue to change, as improved methodologies are developed. As Eric Trist (1981) points out, "We need to know far more than we know at present about the conditions that make for success and the conditions that make for failure. We will have to invent new change strategies for this work." Here are some general indications of where present trends may lead:

- More companies will be devoting more intensive effort to improving the quality of working life.
- Unions will increasingly see advantages in QWL, and North American unions will follow the lead of some European unions in putting pressure on manage-ments to shape QWL efforts to suit the objectives of unions as well as managements, though the Canadian unions are more likely to be ahead of those in the United States. The emphasis on QWL will not, however, alter the basic adversarial labor-manage-ment relationship.
- The QWL specialist will remain a highly skilled, and highly prized, expert, but he will be forced to add more knowledge of engineering and general manage-ment principles to his store of resources. In some European countries, behavioral sci-entists have had to accept a less prominent role in QWL than they perhaps should be-cause they have refused to adapt themselves to the needs of business and to learn the pragmatic language of managers. In North America, many behavioral scientists ap-pear more flexible than their European counterparts, and it is likely that here they will take the lead in developing and broadening the field.

- Government will take an increasing interest in QWL and will succeed in stimulating wider interest, as has in fact occurred in the case of government efforts in the United Kingdom, France, Germany, Canada, and other countries. They will be devoting more attention to it, taking it more seriously, and making more demands on it. The United States will no doubt continue to be an exception in this respect for the foreseeable future, and the diffusion of QWL will suffer accordingly.

One consequence of this will be that we will be seeing the development of broader and more sophisticated methodologies than at present are available, incorporating more considerations of engineering, architecture, and finance. This will include a greater role for technology, and considerably more knowledge will be generated on various technological models that facilitate the design of more types of social systems. Without doubt more ways will be found to design continuing learning into the technology of production and office systems.

REFERENCES*

Bluestone, Irving, 1981. "Labor's Stake in Improving the Quality of Working Life."

Blumberg, Melvin and Gerwin, Donald, 1981. "New Technology–Session I."

Butteriss, Margaret, 1981. "The Organizational and Social Factors Involved in Introducing Office Automation."

Camens, Sam, 1981. "The Implications of Quality Systems for QWL: The U.S. and Japanese Experience and the Unions' New Role."

Cohen Rosenthal, Edward, 1981. "The Impact of QWL on the Union as an Organization."

Edgren, Jan, 1981. "The Scandinavian Experience."

Foster, Joseph, 1981. "How to Get Started—Rohm & Haas (Tennessee) Inc."

Jönsson, Berth, 1981. "Corporate Strategy for People at Work—The Volvo Experience."

Kube, Art, 1981. "Skeena Manpower Project: An Organizational Approach to Solving QWL Problems in a Remote Northern British Columbia Community."

Landen, Delmar, 1981. "Transforming Organizations: Principles and Strategies."

*References are from sessions or papers presented at the QWL and the 80s conference, Toronto, Canada, 1981.

Lynch, Lilian, 1981. "QWL—Communication Workers of America/the A.T.&T. Experience."

Mader, David, 1981. "How Do You Keep It Going? Environment of the Plant."

Mettalia, Joseph, 1981. "How to Get Started—Rohm & Haas (Tennessee) Inc."

Straw, Ronnie, 1981. "QWL—Communication Workers of America/the A.T.&T. Experience."

Trist, Eric, 1981. "Quality of Working Life in the 1980s."

Trist, E. L., et al., 1963. *Organizational Choice: Capabilities of Groups at the Coal Face Under Changing Technologies.* London: Tavistock Publications, 1963.

2
Labor's Stake in Improving the Quality of Working Life

Irving Bluestone

In the play *Fiddler on the Roof,* Tevye, bound by tradition, must face the challenge of changing times and circumstances. He finds himself compelled to grapple with new societal concepts of life as the generation he has helped spawn no longer pays obeisance to his traditions. In a sense, the industrial scene in these "modern times" in the United States is facing a similar challenge as changes in society demand a reassessment of the authoritarian practices of the past and present and influence certain basic shifts in managerial attitudes toward the workers and the structure of the work place.

In the ten-year period from 1970 to 1980 in the United States, for instance, the composition of the work force underwent significant change, and current forecasts presage a continuing transformation.

- Workers completing at least one year of college: blue collar—16 percent up from 7 percent in 1970; service—18 percent up from 8 percent in 1970; white collar—57 percent up from 45 percent in 1970. (Overall, workers today have about four more years of education than was true a generation ago.)
- The nature of the education process has changed, as students are more prone to question the authority of the teacher—even at the grade school level.
- Women as a proportion of the U.S. civilian labor force have increased from 38.1 percent in 1970 to 42.2 percent in 1979. (It is estimated that, in 1980, 53 percent of all women were in the work force and this proportion will rise to 60 percent in the next several years.)
- A recent Conference Board study projects that 86 percent of U.S. families will have two incomes by 1990. There is a constant upward shift in the number of multiple income families.
- Persons age 45 and over as a percent of the civilian labor force have declined from 38.1 percent in 1970 to 30.8 percent in 1979 (to 30.3 percent in 1980).

Daniel Yankelovich, in his widely noted study, *The New Morality*, summed up his findings in part as follows:

> Today's generation of young people is less fearful of economic insecurity than generations in the past. They want interesting and challenging work, but they assume that their employers cannot — or will not — provide it. By their own say-so, they are inclined to take "less crap" than older workers. They are not as automatically loyal to the organization as their fathers, and they are far more cognizant of their own needs and rights. Nor are they as awed by organizational and hierarchical authority. Being less fearful of discipline and the threat of losing their jobs, they feel free to express their discontent in myriad ways, from fooling around on the job to sabotage. They are better educated than their parents, even without a college degree. They want more freedom and opportunity and will struggle hard to achieve it. [1974, p. 37]

It is commonplace to hear business managers anchored in the customary management hierarchical structure — in which the boss makes the decisions and gives the orders, and the employees take the orders and do as they are told — complain that workers today:

- are less attentive to the quality of the product or service in the performance of their job;
- exhibit a surly, cynical attitude toward management;
- run the gamut from apathy to rebelliousness;
- are more prone to unwarranted absenteeism and lateness;
- have no "loyalty" to the employer.

It is evident that these are the imputations of those managers who fail to comprehend the comparatively rapid changes occurring in society and the world of work and who have not yet realized the need to alter their own behavior in relation to their employees. Fortunately, however, an increasing number of business executives have perceived that the old authoritarian mode is not only morally and philosophically incompatible with a society rooted in democratic values, but is moreover antagonistic to their own self-interests.

Furthermore, world competition, not only from Japan and Europe but increasingly from developing nations as well, is compelling a reevaluation of the current system of business administration. Long term planning, the best uses of capital and investment, a review of research and development processes and programs, and the upgrading of managerial skills are some of the aspects of business administration coming under sharp scrutiny. No less so is the vitally important subject of the effective utilization of human resources. Every company proclaims that its employees are its most valuable resource. Most often, however, the proclamation is rhetoric without substance.

A primary function of unions is to make of this proclamation a reality. Toward this end a union represents workers in order to improve their living standards, enhance their job and income security, and establish enforceable negotiated work place rights for them. Essential to the purposes and goals of a union as well is to create a work place climate in which the workers will enjoy job satisfaction derived from recognition of their desire for dignity and self-realization—a knowledge that what they are as adult human beings counts more than being an extension of the tool, and that what they do is intrinsically meaningful.

The process of creating a work life of "quality" embraces those concepts that afford the opportunity for the employees at all levels—middle management, white collar, and blue collar—to be adult citizens in the work place as they are in society. To achieve this objective requires a departure from the all encompassing authoritarian managerial control of the decision-making process; it requires a system in which the employees participate significantly in the process of decision making.

For management this may be a disconcerting development since it represents a challenge to certain long established management prerogatives—especially those relating to decisions over the methods, means, and processes of production or, as the case may be, providing services. Yet the forces of change are impelling business executives to "think anew." For unions these recent developments should be viewed as a further step along the road of unionism's persistent historical goal—to bring a greater measure of democracy to the work place.

For both management and unions, the break with tradition does not come easy. For all that, it is, however, equally apparent that not all traditions are worthy of rigid preservation. From the point of view of the union, embracing the concept of improving the quality of work life raises anxieties, both expressed and latent, that should be thoroughly aired and dispelled.

First of all there is the problem of definition. What, after all, is the quality of working life (QWL)? Definitions abound, and the following are several of them for consideration:

> The essence of QWL is the opportunity for employees at all levels in an organization to have substantial influence over their work environment by participating in decisions related to their work, thereby enhancing their self-esteem and satisfaction from their work. [Greenberg and Glaser 1980, p. 19]

> Quality of work life is neither a single event nor a packaged program. It is a general label attached to systematic programs that involve employees

designing and carrying out improvements in their work conditions. The details vary widely. Sometimes QWL involves representative worker-management problem solving committees or task forces. Sometimes, it involves the creation of worker teams that might take on responsibility for quality control, for distribution of work assignments, and sometimes even for daily supervision.

QWL practices aim at extending growth, challenge, participation, responsibility and control to all employees. [Bell Telephone Magazine 1970, p. 15]

Improving the quality of work life is a people-oriented process dedicated to altering attitudes in the union-management relationship, developing mutual respect between management and labor and a cooperative effort toward achievement and mutually desirable and beneficial goals. Essential to its success is the meaningful involvement of workers in the decision-making process. Its primary thrust is to increase job satisfaction, self-worth, self-fulfillment at work and to enhance the dignity of the individual worker.

Improving the quality of work life is not a substitute for collective bargaining, but it can be complementary to collective bargaining subjects of mutual concern. It may cover a wide variety of non-controversial aspects of labor-management relations. It is not, and must not be, a management gimmick manipulated simply to increase production and profit.

It is essential to establish a relationship of co-equality between union and management in planning, designing and implementing the QWL program.

Fundamentally, improving the quality of work life is rooted in the democratic way of life. To the fullest extent possible, it means that the citizen as worker should be able to enjoy democratic values at the work place in the same sense that he enjoys democratic values as a citizen in a free society. [Bluestone, 1981]

Since QWL is a process derived largely from the unique circumstances existing in each individual situation, the definition will vary with the envisioned objectives. A fairly consistent thread runs through the various definitions, however, namely: the right of the employees to participate significantly in the decision-making process. This is as basic to the concept as it is foreign to the more familiar structure of work organization, and it therefore requires sincere, steadfast commitment on the part of both management and labor.

COMMITMENT TO THE QWL CONCEPT

A prerequisite to change in managerial behavior toward the employees is the commitment to the essential concept of QWL. It is not enough for management at all levels to be persuaded of the need and the justification for embarking on the QWL process. The union at its various levels of authority must likewise be convinced. While the cultural and societal changes described earlier provide motivation for managerial attitudinal change, principles of sound patterns of human behavior should impel it. In fact, however, it is the success of the QWL process where it currently exists that in the final analysis may be the more influential persuader. Concrete examples of vastly increased employee satisfaction through the QWL process and the resultant benefits to management, the workers, the union (and the community and consumers as well) serve to dispel doubts about the value of the QWL concept. In any event, firm commitment to the QWL process at the various levels of the management and the union hierarchies is a primary ingredient for the required initiative, its development, and its success.

COEQUAL STATUS

The constancy of the commitment is best assured within a climate in which both management and the union share coequal status responsibility in planning, designing, and implementing the QWL process. Without the cooperation of management, the union, no matter how deeply dedicated, will find it impossible to initiate, much less fully implement, the program. While management, on the other hand, might succeed in initially installing a QWL program without union cooperation, before long union opposition to such unilateral action will doom the program to ultimate failure. Moreover, a program that is designed and controlled solely by management, even with union acquiescence (but not union support) soon will lay itself open to abuse and exploitation by management itself, since there will be no countervailing force (the union) to protect the workers' interests and preserve the primary purpose of the QWL process: to enhance the dignity of the worker and provide the vehicle for worker self-fulfillment and self-satisfaction at work by assuring that the process remains primarily relevant to the needs of the workers.

SEPARATION OF QWL AND THE LABOR CONTRACT

One of the guidelines that the contracting parties accept as a matter of course when initiating the QWL process is that the negotiated labor contract provisions remain inviolate. Management should not contemplate that the mere agreement to undertake the QWL process through joint, cooperative endeavor means automatic change in the labor contract requirements. Maintaining a clear-cut separation between QWL and the negotiated labor contract is vitally important to both parties and to the workers. This is not to say the parties may not reach the conclusion that "bending" or even modifying certain negotiated contract provisions is desirable under given circumstances. It is up to the parties to the labor contract to reach such a decision, in which case, of course, they have the authority to act on their decision, subject to the usual ratification procedures.

BENEFITS OF QWL

By its very definition, the QWL process is designed for and on behalf of the worker. Its philosophic base, rooted in the principles of democracy and participation, is people-oriented. From labor's point of view, therefore, the QWL process, properly effected, represents an extension of unionism's historic goals.

The benefits that workers and the union derive from the QWL process have also been manifested in other concrete ways—and are benefits of value to management as well.

Improved Product Quality

Workers know a great deal more about how to manage their jobs, and have greater concern for the quality of the product or service, than most managements are willing to give them credit for. If, like automatons, they are simply to be programmed and obey orders, they are deprived of the initiative to respond as problem solvers. As the Japanese system has proven to the chagrin of most industrialized nations, the floodgates of innovation and ingenuity, once opened to the workers, create near miracles of quality service—given the time, the opportunity, and the motivation. They recognize that good quality is tied inevitably to improved job security through assured sales.

It is well established that improved quality is a direct benefit derived from the QWL process—a benefit commonly desired by the workers, the union, the management, and, naturally, the consumer.

Reduced Absenteeism and Labor Turnover

The problem of unwarranted absenteeism is more ofter than not considered an issue solely of concern to management. Obviously, high unwarranted absentee rates are costly, jeopardize continuous high standards of quality excellence, and are disruptive of operations. For the workers who are present, absenteeism often means being moved from jobs that they find desirable to fill in on jobs with which they are not thoroughly familiar. They resent the reassignment and are critical of the union. Habitually absent workers are subject to disciplinary action, even discharge, creating grievance problems for the union representatives. An overall reduction in unwarranted absenteeism rates is desirable from the point of view of the workers and the union as well as management.

Successful QWL programs have demonstrated that increased job satisfaction results in a decline in such absenteeism rates — a mutually desirable objective.

Similarly, labor turnover, costly to management but also troublesome to the union, declines as the work place becomes more conducive to the fulfillment of employees' needs. Reduction in labor turnover makes for greater stability in the work force, which, in turn, makes for a more stable and effective union.

Reduction in Discharges, Disciplinary Layoffs, and Grievance Load

It is a truism that over time the QWL process results in a sharp reduction in the number of disciplinary actions assessed against employees and a notable decline in the number of written grievances. The change in managerial behavior and attitude appears to lengthen the managerial temper fuse; it causes management to seek out the causes of "employee discontent" rather than view only its results. The reasons for the reduction in the number of discharges and disciplinary layoffs may be inexplicable without in-depth research; nevertheless, it is a welcome fact.

The decline in the number of written grievances is attributable essentially to the fact that complaints at the work place are resolved more readily as they arise, through consultation and discussion between the union representative and floor supervision with the grievant. The process of change wrought by the parties' commitment to QWL, influences the collective bargaining relationship. Issues that previously appeared hard core and controversial in nature become the targets of mutual problem solvers rather than problem creators — an altogether salutary development for all concerned.

Election of Union Officials

While it is not universally demonstrable, it is nevertheless a fact that, with few exceptions, union officials who are proponents of the QWL process and are actively involved in planning and implementing the program, are reelected to office. The acknowledged betterment in the quality of working life is the direct result of union effort as a coequal with management. The workers are quick to recognize and appreciate the union's role in bringing a better life into the work place. It is only natural, therefore, that at election time, they will vote for the incumbents who were prime movers in bringing it all to pass. The function of a union representative is to provide service to the constituents and advance their welfare. It is only natural that the constituents in turn support those union representatives who best fulfill that role in their behalf.

Reward System

Job satisfaction, enhanced dignity and self-realization, a feeling that one counts in the scheme of things, is for some reward enough. Financial reward or other types of reward systems may be the handmaiden to a successful QWL process. Profit sharing, gain sharing, paid time off, pay for knowledge, and so on, comprise some of the reward system approaches compatible with the QWL process — usually the subject of the customary collective bargaining procedures. Whatever may be negotiated between the parties will represent a mutually desirable and mutually agreeable pact, which both negotiating parties and the workers consider beneficial.

GUIDELINES

Among the guidelines that the parties might well consider adopting as they enter upon the cooperative process of QWL — over and above the separation of QWL from labor contract provisions and the coequal status position of the parties as noted earlier — are:

- The work pace should not be increased by reason of the QWL program. (Naturally, increased production due to technological change is another matter.)
- The program should be voluntary for all employees.
- The employee should experience genuinely that he is not simply the adjunct to the tool, but that his bent toward being creative, innovative, and inventive, plays a significant role in the production or service process.
- The employee should be assured that his participation in decision making will not erode his job security or that of his fellow workers.
- Job functions should be engineered to fit the employee; the current system is designed to make the employee fit the job on the theory that this is a more efficient production or service system and that, in any event, economic gain is the employee's only reason for working. This theory is, I believe, wrong on both counts.
- The employee should be assured the widest possible latitude of self-management, responsibility, and the opportunity for use of his "brain power." Gimmickry or manipulation of the employees must not be used.
- The changes in job content and function, the added responsibility and involvement in decision making should be accompanied by an appropriate reward system.
- The employees should be able to foresee opportunities for growth in their work and for promotion.

• The employees' role in the business should enable them to relate to the product being produced, or the services being rendered, and to its meaning in society; in a broader sense it should enable them as well to relate constructively to their role in society.

Achieving human dignity by bringing a meaningful measure of democratic values into the work place lies at the heart of the QWL process. And that, after all, is what unionism is all about. The marriage between unionism and its goals on the one hand and the QWL process on the other is a natural culmination of the historic march of labor toward a better life. Labor's stake in the success of the QWL process commands, therefore, that unions be in the forefront of advocacy; that, as has been so often true in the past, they become the initiators, the movers and doers in accelerating the process toward workers' participation in decision making and enjoying the better life.

REFERENCES

Bell Telephone Magazine 1970. "Quality of Work Life on the Bell System Drawing Board," edition 4.

Bluestone, Irving 1981. Unpublished paper distributed for classroom discussion to students in the Master of Arts in Industrial Relations program. Mich.: Wayne State University.

Greenberg, Paul D. and Edward Glaser 1980. *Some Issues in Joint Union Management Quality of Worklife Improvement Efforts.* Kalamazoo, Mich.: W. E. Upjohn Institute for Employment Research.

Yankelovich, Daniel 1974. *The New Morality.* New York: McGraw-Hill.

3
QWL and the 1980s

Eric Trist

Whatever the tasks of quality of working life (QWL) in the 1980s, they will take place in an environment of increasing turbulence—a term that I will explain below. The degree of societal change at present taking place is very great, at least as great as that accompanying the first industrial revolution. We are now well into the second industrial revolution based on information rather than simply energy technologies (Ackoff 1974). The second industrial revolution is being led by the microprocessor—and still newer technologies will doubtless follow—with far-reaching effects on social relations and institutions throughout our societies. We shall, for example, have to give up the idea of full employment, at least as traditionally understood. The recent youth riots in Britain by those of all colors exemplify our unpreparedness to deal with the problems of a partially employed society.

QWL as an international enterprise arose in the early 1970s when the assumption of full employment was still valid. We must continue, indeed intensify and accelerate, all we have been doing since then and are preparing to do now; but during the 1980s we must in addition discover the tasks of QWL in a partially employed society. I will return to this theme toward the end of this chapter.

The societal transition we are in is often referred to as a transition from an industrial to a postindustrial order, though the meaning of postindustrial is far from clear, and there is more than one version of it. But for organizational life it entails in any case moving away from a departing (old) paradigm, with *low* QWL for the many, toward an emergent (new) paradigm, with *high* QWL for the many.

Looking at the increasing rate of change, even as far back as the 1960s, Fred Emery and I (1965) distinguished four types of environment. The first two, where the change rate was slow, need not be discussed in the present context. The third environmental type, called the *disturbed-reactive*, reflects an accelerating change rate and became increasingly salient as the industrial revolution progressed (Table 3.1).

It zenithed some time after World War II when the science-based industries rose to prominence in the wake of the knowledge and information explosions. The best chances of survival in this world went to large-scale organizations with the capacity to meet formidable competitive challenges through amassed expertise. This enabled them to maximize their independent power. The organizational form they perfected was the competitive and singular technocratic bureaucracy in which the ideas of Weber and Frederick Taylor were matched and operationalized to fit the requirements of the disturbed-reactive environment.

The very success of the technocratic bureaucracy has increased the salience of another type of environment, very different from the disturbed-reactive, which is mismatched with technocratic bureaucracy. The new environment is called the *turbulent field* in which large competing organizations, all acting independently in diverse directions, produce unanticipated and dissonant consequences. The result is a contextual commotion that makes it seem as if "the ground" were moving as well as the organizational actors. This is what is meant by turbulence. Subjectively, it is experienced as a "loss of the stable state" as Schon (1971) has put it.

As compared with the disturbed-reactive environment, the turbulent field is characterized by a higher level of interdependence and a higher level of complexity. Together these generate a much higher level of uncertainty. The higher levels of interdependence, complexity, and uncertainty now to be found in the world environment pass the limits within which technocratic bureaucracies were designed to cope.

This means that we must search for an alternative based on a different design principle. Emery (1967) has shown that there are two basic organizational design principles, both of which display "redundancy" in the sense of reserve capacity, as any system must. In the first, the *redundancy* is of *parts*

TABLE 3.1. Change in Organizational Paradigm

From	Toward
A disturbed-reactive environment	A turbulent environment
The redundancy of parts	The redundancy of functions
The old organizational paradigm	The new organizational paradigm
Low QWL for the many	High QWL for the many

Source: Compiled by the author.

and is mechanistic. The parts are broken down so that the ultimate elements are as simple and inexpensive as possible, as with the unskilled worker in a narrow job who is cheap to replace and who takes little time to train. The technocratic bureaucracy is founded on this type of design.

In the second design principle, the *redundancy* is of *functions* and is organic. Any component system has a repertoire that can be put to many uses, so that increased adaptive flexibility is acquired. While redundancy of functions holds at the biological level, as for example in the human body, it becomes far more critical at the organizational level where the components — individual humans and groups of humans — are themselves purposeful systems. Humans have the capacity for self-regulation so that control may become internal rather than external. Only organizations based on the redundancy of functions have the flexibility and innovative potential to give the possibility of adaptation to a rapid change rate, increasing complexity and environmental uncertainty.

This capability makes it imperative to move operationally from the old organizational paradigm toward the new, while the changes taking place in the attitudes and values of the younger generations now in, or soon to enter, the work place make it additionally necessary that a high QWL be available for the many rather than the privileged few. The second design principle makes this possible. These changes are mandatory to ensure our survival at any reasonable economic standard. For we already know that the maintenance of, let alone any increase in, productivity is dependent on scope for human development. This is the central message of QWL.

The shift from the old to the new organizational paradigm represents a discontinuity a shift in the underlying pattern of social values and relations from competition to collaboration. The nature of this shift is shown in Figure 3.1, which is drawn from the work of Cal Pava (1980). In the departing paradigm the overriding governing value is competition; factional warfare of varying degrees limits and constrains collaborative relations. Collaboration is required but is only a subordinate value. In the emerging paradigm collaboration becomes the governing value, which limits and constrains factional competition. Competition is still required, but it now expresses the subordinate value. This is what I mean by a discontinuity.

In a turbulent environment no organization, however large, is powerful enough to go it entirely alone or force its will on others solely by coercion. The interdependencies in which it is implicated are too many. It has to surrender some sovereignty, to share some power. It has to work out with others what I like to refer to as a negotiated order.

In the field of industrial relations this means that labor and management cannot continue in an exclusively adversarial posture in the win-lose mode. Several modes of labor-management collaboration, including QWL, have been accepted for some time in Scandinavia, and codetermination has

FIGURE 3.1. Reversal of Competitive and Collaborative Relations

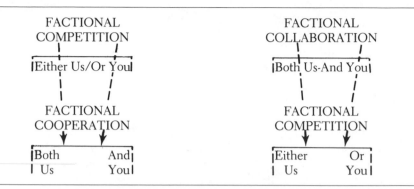

Source: Cal Pava, "Normative Incrementalism." (Ph.D. diss., Univ. of Penna., 1980). This chart is published with the permission of Calvin Pava.

become the built-in way in countries such as Germany. But during the 1970s a collaborative mode began to appear alongside the adversarial mode in countries such as the United States and Canada, where adversarial postures have been a religion—not without some very good reasons. This new collaborative mode has been growing in relation to QWL.

A fundamental condition must be satisfied to permit the growth of collaboration in labor-management relations: the power of labor has to increase vis-à-vis that of management. The more the power balance of the two independent parties approaches equality, the greater the likelihood of their working collaboratively on the unsolved emergent issues on which the welfare of both depends and on which progress to a more democratic form of society also depends. This is a very different story from unions getting in bed with management, or management putting QWL in to keep the unions out. That sort of behavior belongs to the old paradigm.

An example of an early step being taken toward the new paradigm is Douglas Fraser, president of the United Automobile Workers (UAW), going on the board of the Chrysler Corporation. Another is the alternative corporate plan put up by the Combined Shop Stewards Committee of Lucas Aerospace in Britain. Despite stormy initial rejection, this plan not only won some eventual acceptance but lit fires in other prominent British companies that were not doing well such as Vickers and Parsons where many of the stewards' proposals were accepted (Coates and Topham 1980). If one can imagine what would happen much further down the road, it is not entirely fanciful to think that even in North America, collaboration might become primary in labor-management relations, while competition would be reserved for more familiar contract issues. In a turbulent environment the finding of common ground provides the basis of survival for both management and labor and thence of the wider society.

Survival in a turbulent environment depends on human development because it requires innovation. Innovation is necessary to meet the rapid change rate and the rising complexity and uncertainty. QWL operates in the direction of making workers more resourceful and more innovative, therefore more capable and more powerful. Management depends on the increased capability of the work force for the success of the enterprise from which the work force also benefits. This is to put in first place a win-win mode based on collaboration rather than a win-lose mode based on adversarial competition. This competition is still present but now recedes to second place. So long as a disturbed-reactive environment remained salient, the win-lose adversarial mode appropriately took first place. Given the salience of a turbulent field it can no longer remain in first place, which belongs to collaboration.

Let me now look at the attributes of the old and new organizational paradigms as related to QWL. They are summarized in Table 3.2. An account of these issues is given in my paper, "The Evolution of Socio-technical Systems" (Trist 1981a). I need not dwell on them here, but will simply note that a change in these attributes from the old paradigm to the new brings into being conditions that allow commitment to grow and alienation to decrease.

TABLE 3.2. Attributes of the Two Paradigms

Old Paradigm	New Paradigm
The technological imperative	Joint optimization
Man as an extension of the machine	Man as complementary to the machine
Man as an expendable spare part	Man as a resource to be developed
Maximum task breakdown, simple narrow skills	Optimum task grouping, multiple broad skills
External controls (supervisors, specialist staffs, procedures)	Internal controls (self-regulating subsystems)
Tall organization chart, autocratic style	Flat organization chart, participative style
Competition, gamesmanship	Collaboration, collegiality
Organization's purposes only	Members' and society's purposes also
Alienation	Commitment
Low risk taking	Innovation

Source: Compiled by the author.

Equally important is the replacement of a climate of low risk taking with one of innovation. This depends on high trust and openness in relations between management and labor and within both. These qualities are mandatory if we are to transform traditional technocratic bureaucracies into continuous adaptive learning systems.

This transformation is imperative for survival in a fast changing environment. It involves nothing less than the working out of a new organizational philosophy that all the principal stakeholders, including the unions, can voluntarily accept. The transition from old to new will be a slow and difficult evolution as those holding on to the old are going to resist. They will counterattack. They will sabotage. Some of this destructiveness will be unconscious as well as conscious, and therefore more difficult to get at.

A key implication of the list is that QWL projects have to be multi-dimensional. They cannot remain limited to only one or two aspects of organizational life.

There are four main strategic options regarding QWL (Trist 1981b):

- rejection;
- laissez-faire;
- selective development;
- corporate-wide commitment.

Outright *rejection* is becoming less common and is infeasible as a long range position in a turbulent environment. *Laissez-faire* was the most common option during the 1970s. Innovative managers were allowed to go ahead without organizational support, and many projects faded out as a result.

Selective development exists in two versions. In the first, there is no overall corporate commitment to QWL but top management discerns certain work establishments in its purview where it actively encourages QWL projects to be undertaken because it considers success likely and the need significant. This is a pragmatic approach of considerable relevance to large heterogeneous organizations in which different managers and unions espouse different values and have different outlooks. In the second, selective development goes along with overall *corporate-wide commitment.* A QWL philosophy has been arrived at after much consideration, and public commitment to it has been obtained from the principal stakeholders including the union(s). Even with this done QWL projects cannot be started up simultaneously across the board so that the question of site selection again arises. Corporate commitment in conjunction with selective development gives the best chance for QWL projects to endure. This approach is being adopted by such corporations as General Motors (GM) and American Telephone and Telegraph (AT&T). It will, I believe, spread during the 1980s.

Let me now list some of the main tasks that QWL faces in the 1980s:

- To make more completely the shift toward the new paradigm in established as well as new work organizations (where we were rather successful during the 1970s); to go system wide in these organizations and to learn better how to do this; and to find ways of accomplishing diffusion faster. We need more than ever to use the introduction of advanced technology as a lever.
- To encourage independent union initiatives. It is essential that many more unions than the few who have so far done so should take up QWL on their own terms for their own sake, as unions, and press managements to move in the QWL direction — as the UAW did with GM in 1973. Otherwise there will be fewer unions around by the year 2000.
- There is a great need to extend community-based QWL as this makes for synergy and not only yields strong network effects but relates work to other areas of life. Similarly, there is need to extend QWL to the sectoral level, as Einar Thorsrud (1981) has done with the Norwegian Merchant Navy and as the steel industry is doing in the United States, so that wider *problematiques* are addressed that cannot be dealt with at the level of the single organization.
- We need to make greater use of the capabilities of women who are more experienced than men in the intuitive and holistic thinking required to deal with many emergent problems and in the development of nurturant climates necessary to advance our response capability in turbulent environments.
- We need to learn to work far more with small businesses. This was a priority in projects such as Jamestown.
- We need to assist Third World countries in skipping from prebureaucratic to postbureaucratic organizational modes. There is no need for these countries to go through several decades of bureaucratic regimentation.
- There is great scope for developing the use of media such as video tape and film to accelerate diffusion and provide widespread learning opportunities. More communication can become two way and very large numbers of people can be reached.

QWL needs to become related to other forms of organizational democracy. These are shown in Table 3.3 as they are at present distributed among selected countries. These forms all represent modes of participation; they all involve power sharing. Power sharing is at the heart of QWL.

Historically, collective bargaining was the first to emerge; employee ownership, often in the form of cooperatives or (more recently) of firms divested from conglomerates, followed; then came representative democracy with workers on boards, though not sharing in the equity. The work-linked form has been the last to appear. It is concerned with work restructuring and participation at one's own level of decision and is that with which QWL has been most closely associated, as it directly affects the quality of work experience. The four forms have evolved independently, and some of them are regraded as contradictory in certain countries.

TABLE 3.3.   Distribution of Forms of Organizational Democracy in Selected Countries (1980) (on a scale 0–4)*

	Collective Bargaining	Representative	Owner	Work-Linked
Norway	4	3½	1½	2½
Sweden	4	3½	1½	2½
Holland	3	2	1	1½
Australia	2½	1	1	1½
Germany	2½	4	−1	−1
France	2½	1	−1	−1
Britain	4	0	1	0+
United States	2	0+	1	1½
Canada	2½	0+	1	−1
Yugoslavia	0	4	4	0+

*The ratings are personal estimates of the author.

Note: Norway and Sweden exemplify a congruent Scandinavian pattern that Holland and Australia approximate. The larger European countries show no consistency. The United States and Canada express a North American form. Yugoslavia is very different with no independent unions.

Source: E. L. Trist, "The Evolution of Socio-Technical Systems." In *Organization Design and Performance*, edited by Van de Ven and Joyce. (New York: Wiley, 1981). © 1981 by John Wiley & Sons, Inc.

In what may be called the Scandinavian pattern, which Holland and Australia approximate, there is a trend to *confluence*. I would expect the work-linked form, as the only form directly affecting the texture of immediate work experience, to spread in combination with other forms. Combinations of three, if not four forms (though foursomes are beginning to occur in smaller firms), are likely to become more common in more countries during the 1980s. Workers will tend to demand a greater share in the strategic decisions of their ogranizations as they become more self-managing. The means will vary, and there is room for pluralism. In the uncertainty of a turbulent environment people become increasingly uneasy when they are without any degree of control over large decisions that affect their main life chances. The spread of unemployment, the increasing number of mergers, and the shifting of plants overseas will increase these feelings. More workers may therefore be expected to seek representation on boards and participation in the equity of their firms while advancing union strength and restructuring their jobs. Nevertheless many will remain content with the last two, and others will not press even for these.

All the tasks I have mentioned so far are underway to some extent and will proceed during the 1980s in the teeth of opposition from the old paradigm that still has hold on most of the world. But there is a new task: to establish a dissociation between the concept of employment and the concept of work — a consequence of the microprocessor and related technological revolutions. This makes it incumbent upon us to bring into being *a partially employed yet fully engaged society*. As yet, we do not know how to do this. It is a task that requires fresh appreciations. We must legitimate and respect the work that people do when they are not in places of paid employment. We must eliminate their shame and their guilt over not being in such a place. We must assure them a standard of living sufficient for them to take their full place as members of society. We shall have to find some new words, new generative metaphors as Don Schon (1981) calls them, to express the reframing required.

Simplifications and cost reduction are possible in some sections of the engineering industry where layoffs have been estimated at over 50 percent. Word processing is likely to occasion similar personnel shrinkages in many white collar occupations, which will not be able to absorb those made redundant from manufacturing as they did during the first round of automation. Jenkins and Sherman (1979) forecast an overall reduction at 23.2 percent in the British labor force by the year 2000 and identify high risk jobs and sectors. They entitled their book *The Collapse of Work*. The senior author is a major trade union leader. His would appear to be the most comprehensive statement on the issue from a union standpoint. If the present economic slowdown continues the level of employment forecast will be reached by the early 1990s, with women being disproportionately affected.

Simply to shorten the work week by a day, or to propose some equivalent device such as work sharing, or a new norm of working part time are necessary but not sufficient to provide a solution to unemployment on the scale anticipated. This is particularly so when, in addition to microprocessors and industrial robots, further displacement of older industry to the developing world is taken into account. The meaning of work itself will need reconsideration. Sachs (1980), the development economist, has suggested that work in the sense of paid employment will have to be rationed — though it would presumably be possible for the work-addicted to purchase work stamps from the less addicted! In addition to his paid work, an individual would have an occupation in what Sachs calls the "civil society," that is, the community. This concept is consonant with that of the dual economy in which gift and barter arrangements grow up in a "social economy" that exists in parallel with the market economy (Robertson 1981). Transactions in this nonmarket domain may come to equal those in the market domain.

The social economy includes activities that people undertake for themselves by way of self-reliance. They may involve community workshops and many new types of social arrangement. "Jobs" in this area tend to be of high quality and to promote personal growth. They are likely to make the ordinary world of work less central and to make ambition or status in it less pre-occupying than it is at present—at least for some kinds of people. There will be more choices in lifestyles, more types of career path open. Allied to this is a reassessment of the household as a work field that reflects the changing roles of men and women in the domestic sociotechnical system and the links of this system with outside employment. The divorce between home and work, which has been so complete in industrial societies, may be less complete in the postindustrial order.

I will not attempt to go into the question of the decentralization not only of organizations but of society that micro-electronic technologies make possible. They could of course also take us toward greater centralization—to the end of the pier that George Orwell called 1984. The choice is ours. There is no doubt regarding which road QWL bids us take.

I would like to close by briefly mentioning a project in a district of Edinburgh to which I have been going as research adviser during the last five years, as this experience has greatly influenced my search for alternatives (Trist and Burgess 1979). The district is called Craigmillar, which has its own castle where the *haggis* was invented. Nevertheless it is a low income public housing estate where some 25,000 people have lived without amenities in an isolated area on the edge of the city. Industry has gone: the two mines are long closed, and the breweries, except one bottling and distribution plant, have taken off. Unemployment of young adult males varies between 20 percent and 30 percent; for women, unemployment is far higher and too few adolescents have known what it is like to work. Yet this community is at the leading edge of postindustrial innovation and does an enormous amount of work without much in the way of employment.

Some 15 years ago a mother and housewife, called Helen Crummy, was annoyed because her son who had some talent for music could not get music lessons at school. There was no music in the curriculum in such a place as Craigmillar. Voluntarily, they got music lessons going and held a small festival at which local talent could perform. They found they were as good as many other folks. This has led in time to a vast development in community arts that has now become internationally famous. They write and produce musicals and dramas on social issues arising locally and take them touring in the rest of Scotland and in continental Europe.

Their organization is called the Craigmillar Festival Society of which Mrs. Helen Crummy is organizing secretary. Their activities, under local resident control, have transformed a negative into a positive identity. They have gone on to undertake many forms of social service through neighborhood workers, again local residents, who give better attention at lower cost than official departments. They have, with the support of a grant from the European Economic Community, developed a comprehensive action plan for the future of Craigmillar, winning acceptance for many of their proposals from local, regional, and national authorities. They have won a high school and a community center and stopped the planning authority from driving a freeway through the middle of their community.

They have turned a dilapidated church into a community arts center and other buildings into community workshops and meeting places for youth. They have constructed play sculptures for children and have painted bright murals (which have remained unvandalized) in several dull public places.

The jobs in the establishments that have created these amenities, indeed in all Festival Society activities, have high QWL. I have seen many ordinary people grow amazingly in the last few years. Many hundreds have been involved in one way or another, at any given time, making constructive use of government schemes.

All this is work but not employment. What is it if not QWL? The Craigmillar way is one way toward a fully engaged if partially employed society. Moreover, the Festival Society has won the cooperation of several large firms in Edinburgh, who have taken on Craigmillar people because they have become resourceful and committed. A way back to the market place has been opened for quite a few.

The QWL mission is to foster human development through work that is better and more economically done as a result. The QWL mission can be carried out beyond employment as well as within it. Each can reinforce the other.

We must continue to create jobs of high quality and bring into being organizations and communities through the new paradigm that provides the enabling conditions for such jobs to come into existence in both the market and social economies. Otherwise we are not likely to fare too well in countervailing the turbulent environment that increasingly surrounds us.

REFERENCES

Ackoff, R. L. 1974. *Redesigning the Future*. New York: Wiley.

Coates, K. and Topham, T. 1980. "Workers' Control and Self-Management in Great Britain." *Human Futures* 3, no. 2:127–41.

Emery, F. E. 1967. "The Next Thirty Years: Concepts and Methods." *Human Relations* 20, no. 3:199–237.

Emery, F. E. and Trist, E. L. 1965. "The Causal Texture of Organizational Environments." *Human Relations* 18, no. 3:21–32.

Jenkins, C. and Sherman, B. 1979. *The Collapse of Work*. London: Eyre Methuen.

Pava, C. 1980. "Normative Incrementalism." Ph.D. dissertation, University of Pennsylvania.

Robertson, J. 1981. "The Redistribution of Work." *Turning Point* Paper No. 1. Spring Cottage, Ironbridge, Shropshire, Eng.: Private Publications.

Sachs, I. 1980. "Development and Maldevelopment." *IFDA Dossier* No. 2. Nyon, Switz.: International Foundation for Development Alternatives.

Schon, D. 1971. *Beyond the Stable State.* London: Temple Smith; New York: Basic Books.

Schon, D. 1981. "Framing and Reframing the Problems of Cities." In *Making Cities Work*, eds. Morley et al. Boulder, Colo.: Croon Helm/Westview.

Thorsrud, E. 1981. *Work, Home and Education — A New Career Pattern in the Norwegian Merchant Navy.* Paper presented to the Plenary Session on QWL at the Conference of the American Sociological Association, Toronto.

Trist, E. L. 1981a. "The Evolution of Socio-Technical Systems." In *Organization Design and Performance*, eds. Van de Ven and Joyce. New York: Wiley. And as Occasional Paper, Ontario Quality of Working Life Centre, Toronto.

Trist, E. L. 1981b. "The Quality of Working Life and Work Improvement." In *A Reader in the Quality of Working Life.* Ottawa: Labour Canada.

Trist, E. L. and Burgess, S. 1979. "Multiple Deprivation: A Human and Economic Approach." *Linkage* 3:8–9.

4
Social Choice in the Development of Advanced Information Technology

Richard E. Walton

For the past few years, my associates and I have been studying the implications of advanced information technology for white collar work and how social criteria might be employed to guide development in this area. Based on this research, I will suggest why social criteria should be applied, why they can be, and why it is increasingly likely that they will be. Then I will outline some of the issues that arise when we try to apply social criteria.

Extensive automation of white collar work has become possible because of two types of technological advances. The first is an explosive growth in computer power per unit of cost — on the order of tenfold increases every four or five years. The second advance is in telecommunications, making it possible to achieve unprecedented movement and integration of electronic information. Consider also two economic facts: (1) the annual growth rate of capital per employee in offices has lagged behind that in manufacturing, and (2) office overhead costs have risen rapidly in recent years. These factors combine to make an extraordinary variety of new applications economically feasible. Experts regard information technology as the most dynamic sector of technical innovations.

IMPLICATIONS FOR WORK AND PEOPLE AT WORK

My first proposition is that the new information technology has profound implications for the nature of work performed by clerical, professional, and managerial personnel. The potential impact on the work place may be

This paper will also appear in *Human Relations*, forthcoming, and is published here with the permission of Plenum Publications. It was presented both in Plenary Session at the Annual Meeting of the American Sociological Association on 27 August 1981 and as the keynote address at "QWL and the 80's," an international conference on the quality of working life, on 2 September 1982 both held in Toronto, Ontario, Canada.

greater than any earlier wave of new mechanization or automation to hit industry. Thus, I propose that the human stakes are high.

The new technical systems differ from those of prior generations, particularly because their relationship to human systems has become more pervasive and complex—and more important. Earlier systems utilized large computers, performed a limited number of separate functions, relied upon batch-processing, and were tended by special, full-time operators. The newer technologies utilize a network of large and small computers and embrace many activities within a given system, often crossing departmental boundaries. Managers, professionals, and clerical personnel are required to interact *directly* with computer terminals, often as an integral part of their responsibilities. And because these systems are on-line, the relationship between the user and the system is more immediate. Thus, it is not surprising that the newer systems have the potential for affecting more employees in more ways than ever before, and for influencing work and communication patterns at higher executive levels than previously.

Our studies have covered a number of different applications, including the following three:

• Electronic mail terminals were placed on the desks of thousands of managers and support personnel in a large firm. This innovation affected the nature of vertical and horizontal communications, access to executives at different levels, decision-making processes, and it modified somewhat the content of the jobs of those who used the tool.

• A procurement system was installed in a large company, embracing buyers and their clerical support, as well as personnel in the receiving and accounts payable departments. The system made it possible to monitor more closely the performance of purchasing agents, changed the interdepartmental patterns of accountability for errors, and created more tedious clerical work.

• A phone company automated their local repair bureaus, employing information technology to test phone lines automatically, to monitor the status of all repair orders in the bureau, and to provide telecommunication linkage with service representatives at a new centralized office who received subscriber complaints. Before automation, these service representatives were located in the local repair bureaus. Let us look more closely at this application.

In the *repair bureau*, the new technology reduced the number of personnel and decreased skill requirements. The "test man" is a case in point. In the past, being a test man was a professional job, with a high status dress code of "starched white shirts and ties." Mastery required innate ability and experience. Today, the testing function is becoming increasingly automated, and the test man's skills and knowledge have become technologically obsolete. Those holding that position, therefore, have suffered psychologically and economically.

The new system also dramatically affected personnel in the new *centralized answering facility*. The service representatives felt that they had become physically and informationally isolated from other steps in the process of satisfying the customers whose complaints they take. The central facility takes complaints for local bureaus in several states, and the answering personnel neither learn what happens to a particular complaint nor know the people in the bureau to whom they pass along the complaint. Service representatives cannot determine the status of repair work and, therefore, either cannot respond to customers who call back or must provide them with meaningless promises about delivery of services. This has led to tension and mutual fault finding between the service representatives and repair personnel. In these and many other respects the technical system had helped produce "unhealthy" jobs — jobs that failed to meet normal human needs for knowledge and control of the work place. The result was employee alienation and defective problem solving.

Not all of the human side effects of these and other systems we studied were negative. I will turn to that point in a moment. But the negative human consequences we found were significant — and largely predictable. The following behavioral generalizations describe some of the common organizational consequences of office applications of the new microprocessor technology.

If the technical system decreases skill requirements, the meaning of work may become trivial, and a loss of motivation, status, and self-esteem may result. This was a common occurrence, and in some circumstances those who suffered counterattacked the system.

If the system increases specialization and separates the specialty from interdependent activities, then jobs may become repetitive and isolated, and fail to provide workers with performance feedback. Such jobs produce alienation and conflict.

If the system increases routinization and provides elaborate measurements of work activity, job occupants may resent the loss of autonomy and try to manipulate the measurement system. The fact of measurement itself can put excessive pressure on individuals and can strain peer relationships.

IMPACT OF TECHNOLOGY VARIES AND CAN BE INFLUENCED

My second proposition is that technological determinism is readily avoidable. Technology *can* be guided by social policy, often without sacrifice of its economic purpose. Information technology is less deterministic than other basic technologies that historically have affected the nature of work and people at work. True, the side effects described above were generally negative, but sometimes the *unplanned* consequences are positive. In each of the areas listed below, the effects were not inherent in the technology. The directional effects resulted, to an important degree, from particular choices made in design or implementation.

- Work systems based on the new technology often require less skill and knowledge, but sometimes these new systems result in more jobs being upgraded than downgraded. System design can influence that outcome.
- The technical system can increase the flexibility of work schedules to accommodate human preferences, or it can decrease flexibility and require socially disruptive work schedules.
- New systems often contribute to social isolation, but sometimes they have the opposite effect. Similarly, they often separate an operator from the end result of his or her effort, but occasionally they bring the operator in closer touch with the end result. Seldom are these planned outcomes, but they can be.
- These systems sometimes render individuals technologically obsolete because of changed skill and knowledge requirements, but they also open up new careers.
- New technology can change the locus of control—toward either centralization or decentralization.
- New information systems can change—for better or worse—an employee-typist into a subcontractor operating a terminal out of his or her home.

The problem is that those who design applications and those who approve them currently make little or no effort to anticipate their human effects. Thus positive organizational effects are as likely to be accidental as are negative ones.

Why is computer-based technology becoming less deterministic, allowing planners more choice? First, the rapidly declining cost of computing power makes it possible to consider more technical options, including those that are relatively inefficient in the use of that power. Second, the new technology is less hardware dependent, more software intensive. It is, therefore, increasingly flexible, permitting the same basic information-processing task to be accomplished by an ever greater variety of technical configurations, each of which may have a different set of human implications. For example, one system configuration may decentralize decision making; another may centralize it. Yet both will be able to accomplish the same *task* objectives.

TRENDS FAVOR THE EXERCISE OF SOCIAL CHOICE

My third proposition is that a number of factors could produce an industrial trend in which human development criteria would be applied to the design of this office technology. I have not yet observed such a trend. But a social revolution affecting work in the manufacturing plant gathered momentum during the 1970s, and the most natural extension of this social revolution to the office would be a movement to seize upon this new office technology and to shape its development. Managements and unions, where workers are organized, are increasingly acting to modify the way blue-collar work is ordered and managed. And the changes are explicitly in the interest of promoting human development as well as task effectiveness.

The work improvement movement began in the United States and Canada and in some European countries in the early 1970s after several years of sharply increasing symptoms of employee disaffection. Symptoms included costly absenteeism and sabotage, and the media labeled the general phenomenon "the blue-collar blues."

Over the past decade, attention has gradually shifted from symptoms to solutions. Work reform in plants throughout the United States and Canada has grown steadily, and the trend appears to be taking the path of a classical S growth curve. Today, the rate of growth in these experiments continues to increase annually, suggesting that we are approaching the steeper portion of the curve.

Work reform reverses many practices launched with the industrial revolution in which tasks were increasingly fragmented, deskilled, mechanically paced, and subjected to external controls. The current trend combines specialized jobs to create whole tasks, integrates planning and implementation, and relies more on self-supervision.

A particularly striking illustration is provided by General Motors (GM) and the United Automobile Workers (UAW), who have jointly sponsored quality of work life (QWL) activities in over half of GM's facilities. Over the course of a decade, political support for QWL activities within each of these organizations grew to the point where such activities have become the official policy of the dominant coalition within each organization. For GM management, policies that favor human development produce a more committed work force; moreover, these policies have come to be regarded by many managers as morally right. For the UAW, these same policies promote industrial democracy and advance unionism. For the work force, such policies allow some discretion where there had been none; they afford human dignity where it had been absent; and they increase the employees' voice in matters that affect them.

The aims of this social revolution are *not* radical in the sense that they challenge either the ownership structure of industry or the basic legitimacy of professional management's current role in deciding where to allocate resources. In this respect, the social revolution in North America differs from some of the forms of industrial democracy developing in Europe.

Some related North American trends *do* have an impact on the ownership structure of smaller enterprises. Professor William F. Whyte and his colleagues at Cornell University have documented the experiences of firms that have offered employees stock ownership plans. Moreover, the addition of UAW President Douglas Fraser to the Chrysler Corporation's Board of Directors is a step toward labor participation in major decision about resource allocation. But these developments are not typical of the social revolution to which I refer.

The values and behavior patterns that characterize this social revolution have a significance beyond the work place. More research is needed, but the studies with which I am familiar confirm my own observation that when individuals are able to use a broader range of skills and abilities in their work, they tend to see themselves as capable of making a larger variety of contributions to their community. And when people are afforded a voice in or influence over matters that affect them at work, they will expect the same sort of participation in other social settings. In short, human development at work creates pressures on other institutions to promote similar development. Conversely, human constriction at work is conducive to human constriction in other societal settings.

These observations have been illustrated in a number of North American manufacturing plants started in the 1970s where the governing philosophy emphasized human development. Self-supervising work teams were set up that required workers to solve technical and social problems. Members were encouraged to take initiative, to express themselves, and to make constructive use of conflict. The skills and self-confidence gained at work were then exercised in the family setting. For example, their new work roles raised the consciousness of women employees in working class families and many of them undertook to change their decision-making roles at home from passivity to activity and to move their marriage role relationships from subordinacy to equality. Many male workers in these innovative plants practiced their own listening skills at home, again with implications for the human development of family members.

Why did this revolution in manufacturing plants gather momentum during the 1970s? Several forces have led to change, at least in North America. One factor, which I mentioned earlier, was the acute rise in worker disaffection during the early 1970s, not unrelated to the unrest that was occurring in the cities and on campuses. Then during the middle 1970s, it became increasingly apparent that North American industry was losing its competitiveness in international markets. Management looked for better ways to utilize human resources and recognized that it would have to meet more of the employees' needs and expectations. Unions, fearful about the loss of jobs to foreign competitors, increasingly joined in this venture. Recently North American managers, by now somewhat humbled by their own lackluster industrial performance, have adapted Japanese techniques, techniques that also happened to be consistent with quality of work life innovations already developing at home.

No change comparable to that just described is yet underway in the

North American office. Some clerical workers have been the target of quality of work life activities, especially in large insurance and banking organizations. But for the most part there is little activity in this arena. Ironically, where quality of life has been improved for blue-collar workers, white-collar employees in the same facility often feel neglected by comparison. This feeling of neglect is shared by lower level managers and professionals, as well as clerical personnel.

Concern within these white-collar groups is growing, as national surveys confirm a decline in job satisfaction among middle managers. Recently, white-collar groups have found themselves almost as vulnerable to massive force reduction as blue-collar workers. In steel, automotive, and rubber companies, for example, tens of thousands of white-collar employees have been cut.

Management is beginning to recognize that it does not tap the fund of skills and knowledge of these white-collar groups. Recently "quality circle" or participative, problem-solving teams have been introduced into white-collar work places, often with beneficial effects on human development. Still, no major pattern of positive social change has emerged affecting those who work in offices.

It is at this point that new office technology based on the computer-on-a-chip enters the scene. This new technology either can exacerbate the problem of white-collar disaffection or can be part of the solution. Technology can either constrict human development or promote it.

Although not yet constituting a trend, a significant development is the recent agreement entered into by the American Telephone and Telegraph Company (AT&T) and three unions (including the Communications Workers of America) representing 700,000 employees. The unions and the company have established joint committees to discuss plans for new technology at least six months before new equipment is introduced and to analyze the potential human implications, including job pressures and job organization. In Europe there *is* an established trend for companies and unions to enter into "technology agreements," giving unions and employees an opportunity to modify new technology before it is introduced. The AT&T agreement covers unionized employees, who are mostly blue-collar workers, but the idea probably will be extended to the company's white-collar work force as well.

IMPLEMENTING SOCIAL CHOICE

The idea that technology has a social impact certainly is not new. Social scientists have long argued that technology can dramatically affect individuals, institutions, and society as a whole. Managers who introduce new work technologies have long appreciated that there will be organizational side effects. But this knowledge has had little influence on the introduction of new work technology.

In the past, considerations of the human impact of innovation have led merely to efforts to overcome workers' resistance. These efforts have emphasized implementation methods, including communication and training, and employment assurances. But efforts to ameliorate the impact should increasingly extend upstream to the design stage itself, where workers could affect the design of hardware, software, and management-operating systems.

In the past, where human criteria have been considered in the design of work technology, they have centered on narrow factors, such as ease of learning, operator fatigue, and safety. The criteria should be extended to include a broader array of human needs—for autonomy, for social connectedness, for meaningful work, for effective voice.

But in order to exercise social choice in the significant sense I have just described, one must break new methodological ground.

- Organizations need explicit normative models, by which designers can judge what human effects are to be considered good, bad, or neutral, and which ones are especially salient. An organizationally specific model would be based both on general knowledge about human development and on an understanding of the particular circumstances of the company.
- Designs should not be approved until an "organizational impact statement" has been prepared and reviewed. The first step would be an examination of the requirements of a proposed technical system. This would clarify the first order social consequences of the system—how it changes the degree of specialization, locus of control, or skill requirements. The next step would be a prediction of second order consequences, such as motivational effects, social conflict, and human development. This would require the perspectives of behavioral disciplines not currently involved in systems projects.
- One needs practical methods for involving those who will eventually use and/or be affected by a system. While "user involvement" in systems development has been a widely endorsed concept for more than a decade, in practice users seldom report that they have been meaningfully involved.
- Systems development should be approached as an evolutionary process. This contrasts with a more typical assumption that the design can and should be completely conceived before implementation. This methodological recommendation is based on the finding that the human impacts of complex information systems are *dynamic*, in the sense that their effects change over time; for example, some initially negative reactions disappear as tasks are mastered, and some initially positive reactions decline as novelty wears off. Complicating the picture is the fact that effects are *reciprocal* in the sense that the employee will react to the technical system; for example, user reactions may affect the quality of inputs to the system and, in turn, the functionality of the system.

- My final recommendation is that significantly greater effort must be devoted to evaluation of the operational system, and this evaluation must comprehend social effects as well as economic and technical achievements.

These methodological proposals have an additional implication: management should assign a fraction of every development budget to be used to explore the human implications of these systems; then it should act on this knowledge.

We are only beginning to learn how to exercise social choice in the course of technological development. There are still relatively few instances where designers have paid explicit and comprehensive attention to potential impacts on human systems. In Europe there is growing experience with trade unions that have insisted on being involved in evaluating new computer-based technology before it is installed in the work place (Sandberg 1979). Two Cornell professors have developed a model for design and implementation of word-processing systems that attends to social dimensions (Lodahl and Williams 1978). In the United Kingdom, Enid Mumford and her associates have developed a participative approach to the design of systems that affect clerical groups (Mumford and Henshall 1979; Hedberg and Mumford 1975, pp. 31–59). These are pioneering efforts, and though their achievements may be instructive they are by no means definitive.

CONCLUSION

Applications of the new information technology should be guided by human development criteria; they can be so guided and now there is a decent probability that they will be. If this new work technology is to be shaped by social criteria, we will need new implementation "know-how," and a rich field will be opened for basic and applied research.

The design and implementation of advanced information technology pose major organizational problems, and we must deal with the problems. These innovations also represent the most important opportunity available in the 1980s to introduce constructive changes in clerical, professional, and managerial work. First a few pioneering organizations and then a larger number of progressive ones will exploit this opportunity. The introduction of this technology gives us a chance to rethink the organization and management of professional and clerical work in the office that is analogous to the way greenfield plants created an opportunity to pioneer new approaches to managing factory work (Walton 1979).

The 1980s will be a period of trial and error as we learn how to exercise social choice in systems design. Academic institutions can contribute to the analysis and dissemination of these experiences, but only if some managements, systems developers, and unions choose to lead the way in this un-charted field.

REFERENCES

Hedberg, Bo, and Mumford, Enid. 1975. "The Design of Computer Systems." In E. Mumford and H. Sackman (eds.), *Human Choice and Computers*. North-Holland.

Lodahl, Thomas M., and Williams, Lawrence K. 1978. "An Opportunity for OD: The Office Revolution." *OD Practitioner* (December).

Mumford, Enid, and Henshall, Don. 1979. *A Participative Approach to Computer Systems Design*. London: Associated Business Press.

Mumford, Enid, and Weir, Mary. 1979. *Computer Systems in Work Design*. London: Associated Business Press.

Sandberg, Ake. 1979. *Computers Dividing Man and Work*. Stockholm: Arbetsliv-centrum.

Walton, Richard E. 1979. "Work Innovations in the United States." *Harvard Business Review* 57, no. 4 (July–August).

5
Learnings from the Design of New Organizations

Louis E. Davis

The opportunity to define the development of a field that is still dominated by very few theorists and practitioners is rare indeed, especially in the fields of organizational design and the management of organizations. It is a pleasure to have the opportunity, and a deep responsibility, to explore the so far very intimate learnings coming from 30 years of organizational research and 15 years of the design of new organizations. These worldwide experiences provide a basis for optimism that there are developing socially and economically sound organizational alternatives to bureaucracy-scientific management, alternatives that are very much better suited to the realities of the environments of Western societies in the remaining years of the twentieth century. They also generate a deep sense of alarm concerning the slow rate of diffusion of the innovations among managements in Western societies. Large, seemingly impregnable organizations dominant in their past ability to be efficient (short-term success) find that their survival is threatened. Growing numbers of such organizations are demonstrating by their actions that they have lost the capacity to adapt to new, radically different circumstances. This is not the place to examine why organizational renewal was not, and unfortunately still is not in many cases, a central activity of such organizations.

A historical note will provide a context for what is to be reported. What began in the early 1950s as a search for organizational remedies to overcome the then visible defects of bureaucracy-scientific management changed within ten years to experimentation and development of new forms, alternative forms, of organization. By the close of the 1950s, the growing visibility of watershed changes in technology and organizational environment indicated that remedying organization and job structures would likely be insufficient to meet evolving requirements derived from the new path taken by technological development. The threat to organizational survival, now so visible, was then hidden from view. While mechanization continued, it began to be combined with electronic information/decision making, now called automation. Such sophisticated technology began to change what was required of people in order to achieve desired service or product outcomes. Changes in both the content and what is meant by work was accompanied by deep changes, at first unrecognized, in how people could be managed in these new circumstances. By the 1960s it was becoming clear that successful operation of an organization had become directly dependent on the commitment of its members to act appropriately when required. Such settings are now called high commitment organizations. They are characterized by high vulnerability of the organization in its dependence on the commitment of its members. The vulnerability stems from the loss of the conventional means available to the organization of controlling and motivating its members to achieve the organization's goals.

The changes in the environments of organizations that became apparent were those of growing turbulence, seen by some as instability. This concept was first elucidated by Emery and Trist (1965), Vickers (1970), and Schon (1971) as turbulent texture of the environment, the "loss of the stable state," or as environmental instability. Turbulent environments are very slightly, if at all, predictable, limiting severely the reduction of uncertainty surrounding organizations.

In the face of high uncertainty the ability to survive is under great stress. The strategic response of organizational leaders is to make adaptability a principal feature of the organization and thus a design requirement for new (or redesigned) organizations. Operationally, emphasis shifts from conformity with predetermined rules to experimentation and learning to increase response capabilities of the organization and its members. New forms of organization are being tested whose goals are both to be successful (efficient) and to increase learning response repertoires and flexibility of people. Thus the time, disruption, and stress that usually has occurred in making changes to suit new or varying conditions is minimized. In other words the organization is required to have a high adaptive capability. In this instance as well, high commitment is required on the part of the organization's members. Thus there has arisen the unavoidable necessity to design organizational forms and structures and the means of managing them that promote high commitment on the part of its members to the organization's goals.

The learnings about organizations reported here are extracted from new design experiences in both high technology and other settings. Many of these new designs have a high capability of adapting, without distress or disruption, to new and even unpredictable circumstances. As a consequence the learnings reported below are oriented to addressing the realities of the newly evolving era rather than remedying the organizational concepts of bureaucracy-scientific management that arose out of and became synonymous with the fading industrial era.

DESIGN OF NEW ORGANIZATIONS

The most frequent discussion of the design of new organizations, variously called new design or greenfield design, centers on whether such design is less difficult or more difficult to accomplish than change or redesign of existing organizations. Such discussions are instances of both comparing the incomparable and of confusing the amount of time required with difficulty. Both activities are immensely difficult for vastly different reasons. However the crucial issue for the future prospects of enhancing the quality of working life through organizational and job structures, management and union practices, and worker roles lies in the development of tested concepts of organization design. In this regard the experience of the last 15 years indicates that the development and testing of concepts required for building organizations that are both highly effective and provide a high quality of working life are mostly taking place in the design of new forms of organization. Redesign, on the other hand, is providing important new learnings about processes and requirements of organizational change. This chapter is concerned with the former and reports the learnings — some tested, some tentative — derived from new designs. The learnings reported do not fit the academic mold of the social science disciplines. In fact, to approach new forms of organization and jobs the existing mold deliberately had to be disregarded since it is so heavily dependent for its concepts on the long dominant bureaucracy-scientific management models of organization.

The learnings acquired from the designs of new organizations are so extensive and diverse that they touch on most scientific, professional, and practical issues of concern to the structuring and operation of organizations and to the behaviors of their members. They challenge currently accepted wisdom; the cherished truths about management, leadership, control, individual and group behavior, motivation, and rewards, as well as training, recruitment, selection, careers, communication, problem solving, organizational and role structures, and organizational change. New designs that have broken through the accepted organizational mold of bureaucratic-scientific management are providing new insights and data about processes and relationships bearing on organizational psychology and sociology, management, engineering, and architecture. They provide new insights into organizational goal attainment, adaptation, integration, and long-term maintenance. Further, new insights are provided into the influence of technology on structure and behavior, into organizational vulnerability related to advanced forms of technology, and into effectiveness requirements and measurement.

It is difficult to determine where to begin. From a conceptual point of view, one should begin with what seems to be the most important learning, namely the concepts of organizational boundaries and of the basic building blocks of an organization. However, from an application point of view one is led to begin with the development as well as necessity of having available a tested process of design. Thus it may be best to begin with the new organization design process and its requirements. Without such a process it is doubtful that new forms of organization would have been developed and that systematic changes in organizational concepts would have evolved.

Process of Organization Design

The first learning that has become visible is that a different process of organization design is required if more effective organizations having a higher quality of working life are to be created. The new design process uses a different method of reaching design decisions. It is a process strongly based on participation, in which all the participants are required to approach design from a basis of exposing assumptions and concepts with the goal of jointly dealing with the multiple objectives to be satisfied by any organization.

It is a process that integrates world views of leaders, various demands to which the organization must respond, and specific design needs. It promotes the comprehensive view of the organization as a system and as a working society. As such, considerable time as well as support and protection are required to permit exploration of values, acquisition of concepts, and the likely development of alternative world views that may likely challenge the status quo ante. The process also requires the early appointment, at the start of the design, of managers who are to be responsible for the success and survival of the prospective organization. The managers participate in the process of design and are required to stay through the start-up period to assure adherence to the design during implementation. Lastly, to assure continuity, those appointed to the design team and then to manage the organization should be mature, confident individuals who understand themselves and do not need to rely on the power and status of their roles or on control mechanisms as crutches or protection of their positions.

The notion that a deliberate process of organizational design is required is in itself a new development, since no such identifiable process had existed earlier. The "design of organization" was a matter of fitting specific needs into the precast bureaucratic-scientific management mold which made design synonymous with drawing an organization chart. The major contribution that can now be reported is that since the early 1970s, a deliberate, systematic, structured, comprehensive process of organization design, tested in a number of complex applications, has become available. To date the process has been only partially reported (Davis 1982).

The organizational design process, as does the process of redesign, brings together diverse and often conflicting interests and professionals whose contributions are needed if both a comprehensive and systematic design is to be completed. Each has a specific role to play in the process. The diverse contributors are brought together on the basis of the structuralist concept of organizational performance and behavior. Briefly stated it is that the structure of the organization (roles and relationships) and climate or environment influence to a very substantial degree, by response to requirements and/or constraints, the behaviors of the organization's members and their responses to either organizational goals or parochial goals.

The roles that the diverse participants play in the design process include not only the provision of deep technical knowledge in their own areas of expertise but also the open interactions among what each perceives as necessary requirements to be satisfied. The consequent and necessary clash between competing and/or opposing world views, their correlated concepts and perceived needs, and the conflicts that emerge provide the basis for examining the likely divisive impacts on the prospective organization. Failure to examine and resolve the divisive impacts will likely lead to suboptimal performance of the organization and unsatisfactory consequences for its members. The participants in the design process come to understand in significant ways that joint optimization based on joint design of all the features and functions of the organization provides the basis for resolution of conflicts over design choices. It is here that the potential resides for innovation of new organizational forms, managerial practices, and worker roles.

The process of integrated comprehensive design has sometimes been called organization-plant design (Lawler 1978; Davis 1979) because it includes the design of the (1) technical (transformation) system and its accompanying work system, (2) physical facilities, (3) buildings, (4) organization structure, (5) job design, (6) careers, (7) rewards, (8) training, (9) recruitment, (10) selection, and (11) adaptation (organization change) mechanisms. Perhaps most important is the world view embodied in the process that the organization is a small or mini-society. Only by designing the above aspects jointly will systemic social and technical requirements for achieving outcomes (goals) be met optimally. Jointly designing the various technical and social systems generates opportunities for meeting the joint objectives of high organizational effectiveness and superior quality of working life.

The design process begins in a threefold manner by (1) negotiating with the leadership of the enterprise, agency, union, and so forth, their expectations regarding design outcomes to be achieved, (2) establishing a temporary structure for carrying on the process of design (which lasts until the design or redesign is concluded and the new design is activated), and (3) requiring the top management and union leadership (where there is a union) to consider and agree on a shared view of the future facing the organization and the social and economic values that will guide the design process and the subsequent operation of the new or changed organization. Agreeing on shared futures and values requires a carefully designed exercise. The outcome of the exercise leads to development of "internal social policy" that is reported as a "statement of organization philosophy" (Hill 1972; Davis 1980b).

Temporary Design Structure

The temporary structure needed to carry on the organizational design process is indicated in Figure 5.1.

The temporary structure is sometimes two tiered and at other times three tiered depending on technical complexity. In the latter instance design sub-teams may be required. Important to successful design outcomes are the method of operation and scope of activities of the design team. The

FIGURE 5.1. Organizational Design Process: Stages and Structure

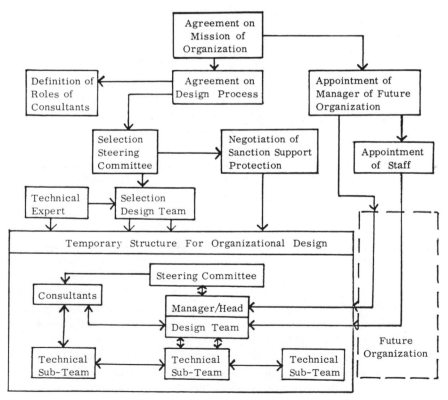

crucial feature is that only the design team as a *whole* may make the final choices or design decisions regarding the various features of the organization and its technical system. The various technical, managerial, and social experts who are members of the design team have the dual roles of both advising and deciding instead of their former experts' unilateral design decision powers that are now the property of the design team as a whole.

The scope of activities of the design team are unlimited within the bounds of money, product, social and other policies laid down by the steering committee. The scope includes the design of the production process, equipment, information systems, organization structure, job designs, career paths, measurement and control systems, advancement, rewards, selection, training, discipline, and so forth. In brief, the scope includes all aspects of the creation and maintenance of a work society, its tools, equipment, and physical facilities.

ORGANIZATION PHILOSOPHY

A second crucial learning is that neither organizational design nor technical design can proceed without agreement on the social values that will guide the new organization or society that is being created. Developing a statement of organization philosophy is the first order of business in the process of organizational design following the creation of the steering committee and design team. As such the difficult task of elaborating and agreeing on values becomes the earliest activity of the design team and steering committee. The new process of design makes explicit values or organization philosophy, referred to by some as the superordinate goals of the organization (Pascale and Athos 1981). Its impact on design is pervasive for it serves both as goal and guide and is a visible reminder that the designers are providing an answer to the question "What kind of society are we proposing to build?"

To recapitulate learnings, what appears to be absolutely crucial is that there is agreement on a basic set of predesign requirements that must be satisfied if design of new organization is to take place (in contrast to copying). These requirements concern (1) elucidation and agreement on values that will undergird the prospective organization, (2) the use of a process of joint design, (3) establishment of a supportive design structure, and (4) negotiation and agreement on the scope of the process and the authority of the design team. What has been learned is that innovative design is not likely to take place, perhaps cannot take place, unless a deliberate joint design process is established.

A number of things are essential for the process to function. There has to be an agreement on values or superordinate goals, embodied in an organization philosophy statement. A temporary design structure has to be created for the duration of the design period to provide integration and resolution of conflicting requirements and demands. The scope of the design activities has to be negotiated to bring within the purview of the design team all aspects of organization structure and operation. Organizational innovations are not likely to be developed without inclusion of the design of technical as well as social systems. The authority of the design team has to be negotiated so that all design decisions are under its control and the implications of all technical, economic, and social decisions will be jointly explored as a basis for making optimal choices. Lastly, top management, through a steering committee, has to provide sanction, support, resources (particularly time), and protection for the design team so that it is able to develop innovative outcomes.

ORGANIZATION ENVIRONMENT

The design of a new organization — the creation of an institution where none existed before — makes very clear that what is being designed is the organization as a complex of four interacting entities. These four entities are described as follows:

- A *transforming agency* that converts provided resources into desired products or services; a place where work is done; and a work organization created to achieve those desired outcomes whose accomplishment requires the creation of the organization in the first instance.
- An *economic entity* that uses resources and has the responsibility of accounting for them to private or public sources.
- A small *society* in itself that provides to its members rewards, identities, valued relationships, continuity, socially valued roles, and association with the larger society of which it is a part. As a mini-society, the organization acquires the supplementary goal of survival or permanence.
- A *collection of individuals* whose membership in the organization provides the means for satisfying a variety of individually different social and personal goals and expectations. In Western societies with their emphasis on individualism, the means and process provided for satisfying some if not all of the individual's goals and expectations are key to the individual's commitment to the organization's goals.

The design of a new organization reveals that multiple goals exist whether or not they are formally recognized. There are many stakeholders inside and outside the prospective organization, and they generate a multiplicity of goals and expectations to be satisfied. This is what is implied in the statement that the organization is an open system — open to the influences of and having to meet requirements originating in its environment.

Design in the present turbulent environment requires concern not only for success (economic and technical efficiency) but for organizational survival (Emery and Trist 1973). Given unpredictability and irreducible uncertainty the survival goal introduces the necessity of designing highly adaptive organizations, with a concomitant shift in emphasis from internal stability to continuous change. For the designer this brings the requirement of creating an organization that can learn from its experience and continuously change while doing its work and meeting its goals. Great emphasis must be given to the design of effective mechanisms for learning, adaptation, and renewal (redesign). Carried in train are issues of levels of information and feedback that enhance learning, adaptation, and renewal. Lastly, roles for the organization's members that will develop flexible people who can support organizational adaptation have to be designed. It is out of the attempts to satisfy these new requirements that are coming the new (nonbureaucratic-nonscientific management) forms of organization.

ORGANIZATION STRUCTURE

Perhaps the most significant set of decisions to be made in designing an organization concerns the internal structure—how to divide up the organization or more specifically where to put the boundaries. Conventional wisdom informs us to place boundaries so that like functions are grouped together, sometimes referred to as organizing by similar technology, or functional organization. This dominant proposition of bureaucracy-scientific management has acquired a vast mythology, largely unverified, extolling the benefits of placing like functions together. The belief has become organizational dogma to be taken on faith with short shrift to any challenger. This proposition is bolstered by two others; place boundaries so that activities performed in the same time period are grouped together and/or those performed in the same locale are grouped together. These have come to be known as organizing by time (shift) and/or place.

Boundaries

At this moment, very likely the most significant learning from new designs concerns how to locate organizational boundaries. Placing boundaries is very likely the most crucial single act in the design of an organization. Boundary location influences almost all else in organizational structure. It directly affects the units of the organization that are created by the partitioning, influencing what responsibilities are to be assigned to the units. Relatedly it influences what are appropriate information, control, measurement, and feedback systems, and what will be the basis of interpersonal and intergroup relationships. Inappropriate boundary location largely influences both the number of organizational levels required and management style, and thus the type of managerial skills required. Practical application of the learnings concerning boundary location confront the dilemma that boundaries cannot be located without prior choice of *what are to be the "basic building blocks"* of the organization. Making this choice in turn depends both on the organizational philosophy and on chosen technology (Miller 1959).

For the present, the learnings about boundary location have been stated as a set of guidelines or propositions for the designer of organizations.

> Boundary Location: Locating internal boundaries determines the composition of self-maintaining organizational units. Boundary location is a crucial early activity in organizational design. The choice of boundaries can facilitate or impede the achievement of many organizational objectives. Internal organizational boundaries should be located so that:
>
> (a.) Within an organizational unit, those responsible for achieving the outcomes can have access to and exercise control over the disturbances or variances that occur in performing work.
>
> (b.) Members of a unit can develop some autonomy or a substantial degree of control over their own activities in achieving the desired goals of the unit.
>
> (c.) Members of a unit can have access to all the information they need to solve the unit's problems and to assess its performance (feedback).
>
> (d.) The boundaries are between the main transformation processes rather than cutting through a process.
>
> (e.) They are at the completion of a process, product, or subdivision of the product.
>
> (f.) The outcomes of work activities can be measured at their boundaries in order to provide feedback needed by the members of the unit to regulate themselves.
>
> (g.) Members of a unit can develop an identity with the product, process, or outcomes.
>
> (h.) Coordination between activities and people can be accomplished within the organizational unit, leaving integration to boundary managers.
>
> (i.) Members of a unit can develop face-to-face relationships in carrying out the work of the unit.
>
> (j.) The requisite skills and activities needed to perform assigned work and to maintain the technical and social systems of the organizational unit are within the boundary.
>
> (k.) The need for external control and external coercion is minimized. Increased opportunities are available for self-regulation in achieving desired outcomes. [Davis 1982, Sect. 8]

Organizational Building Blocks

Many of the options available in organizational design become constrained by the choice of its units of organization or the organization's "basic building blocks." Without regard to changed circumstances, values, and technology, the most widely used unit at present is still that called for by bureaucracy-scientific management, namely one person plus his or her task in a specific time period (a work shift). Organization designs using such units are required to be careful to separate the contents of task-job activities of each unit or person. Carefully drawn job descriptions formally assuring such separation become a concomitant requirement. The results are well known: built-in incapability to cooperate and inhibition to learning. Not infrequently informal cooperation and learning are rewarded by punishment. Rigid job demarcation leads to a "it-is-not-my-job" syndrome. In placid, less demanding times, the price for all this was somehow affordable. However, the person-task per shift building block brings with it suboptimization, organizational rigidity, and inflexible people resulting in incapability to adapt. Lack of adaptability in a turbulent environment is nonaffordable for it carries the frightening potential of nonsurvival.

New designs have been particularly useful in identifying the characteristics of organizational units. Ideally it appears that the basic building block of an organization should be a miniature version of the organization of which it is a component. As such the unit can discharge the responsibilities assigned to it by carrying on its activities in much the same way as the larger organization. In this sense an organization is made up of miniature organizations, each responsible for a service, process, or product outcome. Such units have been called self-maintaining organizational units and have been described as follows:

> Adaptive organizations require self-maintaining units as their basic building blocks. A self-maintaining organizational unit is one that has the capability to perform all the activities required to achieve its specific objectives under a wide variety of contingencies. It can maintain its internal structure and adapt itself to changing demands impinging upon it from its environment. Such units may exist as groups with supervisors — semi-autonomous teams, or without supervisors — autonomous teams. [Davis 1982, Sect. 8]

Self-maintaining organizational units cannot be too large, although successful ones are operating that are much larger than previously indicated by small group theory. This is so even when the units are in the form of autonomous teams without supervisors. The units cannot be any smaller than four or five or they are too easily disrupted by such events as promotion or absenteeism. Successful units of 25–28 exist; however, they have taken very much longer to develop group cohesion than groups of 14–18. Such units provide the basic ingredients for the organizational adaptation and renewal more frequently needed at present. Partially this is based on the very considerable learning that takes place, particularly learning at the system level as well as at the job and task levels. Additionally there is direct experience with system level problems and with problem solving, as well as wide knowledge of organizational issues. All this leads to an identity with the wider system or the larger organization.

Self-maintaining units as the basic building blocks require less direction, less coordination, less dealing with problems they export, and as such require less supervision and fewer levels in the hierarchy. Contributing to the need for fewer supervisors and hierarchical levels are the substantially larger size of the units than the small groups resulting from the small (seven) bureaucratic span of control, and the tendency of the units to become self-regulating within the limits of given responsibilities and resources.

TECHNICAL SYSTEMS

For the practical world of application, the learnings derived from the relationship between technology and organizational design are perhaps the most profound. They call for new commitments on the part of top management, the sanctioners of new design or redesign, and new skills on the parts of both technical and organizational designers. Beginning with the application of technology itself, what becomes very evident is that many technical systems can be derived from a single technology and it is the technical system as designed that has the direct effect on the organizational and job structures. First, there are choices of technical system that raise the considerations of who should make the choices and what policy, principles, or desiderata should guide the choice-making process. Second, the response to these considerations is totally affected by an additional learning, namely, that technical system design cannot in fact be completed by technical designers without basic social system considerations. The process of designing a derivative technical system from a technology requires the designer to answer the question, "How will the machine or system be operated and controlled?" In the present and usual approach, the technical designer decides who will do what with the machines and system and how these will fit into the overall functioning of the process or product system. These decisions are of course organizational design decisions that are already foreclosed when most conventional new design or redesign begins. Seen from the point of view of satisfactorily designing technical systems, technical designers are, either unknowingly or reluctantly, "social system engineers." Thus we begin to understand why when we import or export a foreign technical system we also import or export with it the cultural or social assumptions of the country of origin. The twentieth century belief that science and technology are free of social values can be seen to be a myth that has had enormous negative consequences for Western societies. Returning to practical application, realities and not myths have to be met.

The above learnings have led to two significant positions. The first is that technological determinism is a put-off, if not a sham. It is a defensive posture adopted by those who either have no policy or desiderata to guide them or who are incapable of delving into the deep technical and social issues that have to be confronted in technical system design. In relation to the latter, the concepts of sociotechnical systems provide significant contributions. The second learning is that the process of technical system design and organizational design cannot be permitted to take place independently or even separately from each other. The crucial decisions to be made depend on joint considerations. So one of the most visible outcomes based on learnings from new designs is the creation of a process of organizational design embodying joint design of the technical systems and the social systems of the organization. Among other considerations organizational design encompasses the process of embedding the technical system within the social system. The new process of design can be expected to spread widely because it addresses reality, aids technical designers in areas where they have been very uncertain, and addresses issues brought by the profound changes in the texture of organizational environments. Furthermore, what has been learned from new designs is not exclusive to new designs. The redesign, modification, or renewal of existing organizations has to deal with all the issues facing new design but must do so in the face of constraints, whether small or substantial, coming from the history of the existing organization.

New designs, because of economic considerations, make more visible the trend of independent isolated design of technical systems in the direction of "high technology" or automated systems. These more than highly mechanized systems are composed not only of sophisticated mechanisms such as are found in assembly robots, but they are interlocked or integrated and kept within acceptable control limits by computer and microprocessor-driven devices. Such high technology or automated systems severely change "how the machine or system will be operated and controlled," which is the relationship between people and machines or machine systems, and so change the meaning of work. The focus of the work system moves from interaction with machine to system and from predictable actions to those drawn from a wide response repertoire in response to unexpected events interrupting system continuity. This redefinition of the contents and purposes of work and the requirements of the work system were first described in 1971 (Davis 1971). More and more frequently what emerges from technical system design is the necessity to provide a "high commitment organization." When technical system design is undertaken in isolation, organizational designers are not even aware of the new requirements they create until much too late. A high commitment social system is one that has been (or needs to be) designed to achieve and sustain high commitment to organizational goals on the part of the organization's members so that the technical system can be effective, that is, maintain high continuous capacity permitting economical achievement of service or product goals.

The design of high commitment organizations simply cannot be achieved unless joint design is undertaken so that the needed bases for building members' high commitment become part of the design requirements of both the technical and social systems. There is no evidence that high commitment can be developed through the design of social systems alone no matter how innovative these may be. In addition to the lack of access to technical system choices and thus to the underlying requirements of the work system, existing conventional wisdom regarding worker motivation is simply inadequate for dealing with the requirements of high technology. The consequences of incorporating high commitment requirements are not only different technical system designs but organizational structures radically different from the forms and precepts of bureaucracy-scientific management. Such structures are still in the process of development and at present are known as alternative forms of organization (Davis 1977). The exploration and experimentation with alternative organizational structures is at the core of innovative organizational design.

SOCIAL SYSTEMS

In general social systems are the structures, roles, relationships, and functions of groups and individuals directed at the operation of the organization in its various manifestations as a transforming agency, economic entity, small society, and assemblage of individuals. More specifically, reflecting the new organizational design experiences, the general definition of social systems as used here is modified to describe both the organization and its constituent units as social systems. In the most advanced of the new organizational forms, the social system of an organization is a structure consisting of a set of mini-organizations or mini-societies based on an espoused set of social values, an organizational philosophy. They are tightly integrated by a variety of lateral and hierarchical mechanisms specific to providing a role for all the mini-societies in the goal attainment, adaptation, integration, and long-term maintenance functions of the organization, their larger society. Similarly the social system of a constituent organizational unit is a set of individuals tightly integrated by lateral and hierarchical relationships and by agreed to social values who have roles within and across the boundaries of the units. The roles of each member encompass elements of all activities of the unit and of the larger organization as well as activities focused on the members of the unit as individuals. Learnings from new designs about social systems of organizations follow.

Social System Structures

At the level of the organization as a social system, success (effectiveness) and survival seem to be related to those social system structures that provide:

• Open, visible relationships between managers and the organizational units and their members concerned with decision making, action taking, goal setting, justice, power, status, and rewards. Some have called this demystification of management. It is more than that, as it is also considerably more than communication for it involves sharing of functions, participation in decisions affecting the units and their members, and open flow of all useful information to provide advance knowledge as well as feedback.

• Participation of organizational units or their representatives in goal attainment functions, particularly in goal setting and in organizational control functions including evaluation and measurement.

• Participation of the organizational units or their representatives in the functions concerned with integration and coordination of the organizational units.

• Both on-going organizational adaptation mechanisms such as organization-wide standing change committees, and the participation in them of organizational unit representatives. In effect, what exists is a participative continuing process of change making as a visible everyday activity.

• Both on-going norm setting mechanisms and the participation in them of organizational unit representatives. Such mechanisms provide the shared means for setting acceptable standards of behavior and acceptable practices. In sum, both the mechanisms and the participation stimulate learning and understanding of environmental requirements, and complex problem solving. Everyone in the organization comes closer to the realities of organizational survival.

Organizational Philosophy

Social systems cannot be designed without an espoused set of organizational social values. The values concern the relationship of the organization to the larger society, the responsibilities it undertakes in relation to its members as individuals, its positions on status and individual differences, and so forth. These value statements and others serve both as superordinate goals and as design guidelines. The first stage in the process of design usually is the development of a statement of values as an organizational philosophy.

Joint Design

Only suboptimal social systems will result if design is limited to choices remaining after technical systems have already been designed in isolation. Where technical systems depend for success on high commitment social systems, joint design of technical and social systems becomes an absolute necessity. This is particularly the case if requirements for achieving high commitment are to be provided.

High Commitment

The differences between developing commitment and developing motivation are very substantial in terms of characteristics of a social system. In high commitment settings where what has to be done is not specifically known and when the need to act cannot be predicted, that is, they are substantially randomly determined, then appropriate self-initiated action is crucial to success. What are the requirements for appropriate self-selected, self-initiated action, i.e., high commitment of the individual to the goals of the organization? So far learnings from new designs indicate that the requirements include provision of the means for jointly satisfying both the organization's and individuals' goals. The commitment of the individual to the organization's goals increases with opportunities to satisfy some, if not most, of individual's goals and expectations. In aid of joint goal satisfaction, a social system is required that is sensitive to individual differences, opportunities for participation, learning, advancement, choice, self-regulation, and this assures justice and equity.

Quality of Working Life

High quality of working life is a fundamental consideration in organizational design if social systems are to be effective in the 1980s. Quality of working life means the quality of the relationship between employees and the total working environment, with human dimensions added to the usual technical and economic dimensions.

Enough has been written about the present societal environment to indicate why attention to achieving high quality of working life is essential to organizational effectiveness and survival (Davis 1980a; Yankelovich 1981). Needless to say, high quality of working life is one of the bases on which is built the individual's high commitment to organizational goals. High quality of working life is part of an organization's social policy or organizational values and is so indicated in its statement of organizational philosophy. Where an objective of organizational design is to provide a high quality of working life, it does not imply that everyone wants the same values from a work situation and therefore options should be provided to accommodate individuals' preferences.

The important general criteria for high quality of working life, based on a variety of studies, are:

security;
equitable pay and rewards;
justice in the work place;
relief from bureaucratic and supervisory coercion;
meaningful and interesting work;
variety of activities and assignments;
challenge;
control over self, work, work place;
own area of decision making (or responsibility);
learning and growth opportunities;
feedback, knowledge of results;

work authority — authority to accomplish that for which one is held responsible;
recognition for contributions — financial, social, and psychological rewards, status, advancement;
social support — can rely on others when needed and be relied upon, can expect sympathy and understanding when needed;
futures that are viable (no dead-end jobs);
ability to relate one's work and accomplishments to life outside the workplace;
options or choices to suit the individual's preferences, interests, and expectations.

Careers

Effective social systems include not only the design of work systems but of career structures for all members of the organization. Alternative career opportunities and particularly participation in career choices are essential both to high commitment and to flexibility (adaptation) of individuals. Alternative organization designs indicate that further learning is needed concerning the structuring of careers in organizations based on teams and few layers of supervision and management.

Adaptability

The capability of the social system to adapt seems to be related to the structure of the organization, units or groups and individual jobs or roles. At the organizational level there are established standing groups or committees that recommend changes providing the adaptation function of the organization. Their membership is drawn from the various organizational units and levels. They are permanent entities continuously engaged in capturing organizational learnings and recommending organizational changes, and not temporary or ad hoc groups thrown together to help deal with an emergency situation. Included in structural design is the design of organization-wide systems of information and feedback providing information to all units and levels based on the sociotechnical systems principle of making information available at the lowest level in the organization needed for decision making (Cherns 1976). What is seen in such designs is the open flow of all kinds of information relevant to discharging of individual and joint responsibilities of groups or teams and their members.

Basic to building adaptability is the choice of self-maintaining groups or teams as the basic units (building blocks) of the organization. Such units, based on the principle of multifunctionalism (Cherns 1976), have within them most, if not all, of the skills and work authorities needed to carry on the work of the units. They have available all the information and feedback required for their own activities and for the units with which they interact. Further, they have the means to continually exchange information, problems, and plans with related units and levels of the organization. Internally teams make learning readily available to their members and provide both financial and status rewards for learning. The most adaptable teams appear to be those that have a flexible internal structure by means of minimization, if not removal, of job boundaries. In such units the work to be done belongs to the team as a whole and the team's responsibilities are shared by all members. Who does what when is decided by the team, depending on changing circumstances. The teams engage in problem solving and improvement activities to enhance their abilities to achieve their goals.

Individual members of the organization's units have substantially comprehensive roles requiring wide repertoires of responses. They participate in work, problem solving, and improvement activities and exercise substantial self-regulation in their work assignments. Their knowledge of the state of affairs in their teams and organization wide is very large, permitting effective participation in change (adaptation) activities.

Teams

Implementation of self-maintaining organizational units as basic building blocks has led to the extended development of teams that are both autonomous and semi-autonomous. What defines a team, as distinct from a work group, is that its members share the responsibility for achieving common objectives or goals. A work group, on the other hand, is one whose members share a set of social or authority relationships through reporting to a common supervisor. Although its members may have additional relationships, they do not share the responsibility for achieving a common goal or objective.

It is not clear yet whether autonomous teams, without supervisors, or semi-autonomous teams, with supervisors, are more adaptable to changing requirements imposed by an unstable environment. Effective teams, including self-regulating teams, exist that are larger in size than small group theory has indicated. They range in size from five to twenty-eight members and are more effective in discharging their responsibilities provided they can maintain their self-regulation, which requires that supervision or management provide boundary protection. A very significant learning is that if self-maintaining units are to be effective, their members require competencies in addition to the usual work skills. These have come to be known as social system skills, by which is meant skills in communicating, self-management, conflict resolution, counseling, and developing social contracts. Acquisition of such skills requires additional and new kinds of training.

For autonomous or semi-autonomous teams to survive certain requirements must be instituted and maintained. One such requirement is that the work required to discharge a team's responsibilities belongs to the team as a whole and the team assigns work to its members on the basis of competence and other factors. Another is that inputs to a team are controlled by it if it is to be responsible for outcomes. A third requirement is for an open flow of information to and from each team, coming from management and other teams; and that its own actions and teams play a deliberate part in the information (feedback) transmission process.

MANAGEMENT

The various new forms of organization with their different structural arrangements lead to altered roles for supervisors and managers. The altered roles emphasize a major shift for managers from directing, assigning, controlling, problem solving, and so on at the center of their organizational units to performing these functions at the boundaries of their units. Boundary management cannot take place unless managers provide for members of their units the competences needed for them to carry out most of these functions as a team. Supervisorial and managerial roles are restructured to support boundary management. Such management provides buffering or mediation of changes in the environment so that the units are not upset as they carry on their work. The language used by supervisors and managers in these new forms of organization reflect their changed roles. Often heard is: "I can now plan ahead and avoid spending all my time fighting fires." "I can now get out of the trenches and see what is coming and plan ahead so that my people and I are not inundated and always digging out."

The altered roles call for managerial supportive functions to be undertaken. One function is the building of broad and appropriate response capabilities within the units to meet expected external demands. This requires enhancing competence of the units' members through training and experience. A second function is allocating needed resources to be used by units as required in support of achieving their goals. A third is auditing of units (teams) performance to provide feedback and support. A fourth is evaluation of units' accomplishments rather than the behaviors of their members. A fifth function is developing participation in setting goals and standards, and a sixth is developing problem-solving capabilities in the units.

Managers exercise leadership and control so as to further strengthen and maintain the units (teams). Measurement and evaluation approaches are developed that suit managing by objective outcomes (results achieved) instead of by behaviors displayed. Similarly, there is greater investment in training and in developing wide response repertoires of members, and in providing training and time for team problem solving. Managers control organizational units (teams) rather than directly controlling each individual employee.

CONCLUSION

There are effective methods of organizational design that overcome holding the structure of organizations and jobs hostage to independently designed technical systems. The most effective approach available now is that of joint design based on sociotechnical systems concepts wherein the technical and social systems of an organization are designed interactively.

The process of design of new organizations makes visible viable and effective new or alternative forms of organization (Davis 1977). These are organizations consisting of integrated self-maintaining organizational units that are structured and supported to act as self-regulating mini-organizations (mini-societies).

The alternative forms of organization are much more responsive to external uncertainty and instability and within limits are highly adaptive. They have great capacity to change in large and small ways. These organizations have developed flexible and informed members and joined them into cohesive units bound together by shared rather than imposed values, by high commitment, and by participation in a wide variety of functions required to achieve goals, maintain the organization, and deal with short- and long-term problems. The responsiveness to changes in the environment is supported by different supervisory and managerial roles that grow out of managing self-maintaining organizational units. In such units (teams) members perform short-term control, coordination, and change. Integration of the units (teams) and long-term planning or steering of the organization in relation to its environment receive the time and attention needed by management. Yet to be learned is whether the alternative forms of organization can develop adaptability sufficient to the very large changes confronting organizations and their job holders for the rest of this century.

There is widespread belief that alternative forms of organization are very fragile and therefore will not survive. This is not so. The few that have failed to survive have left valuable lessons behind. Most important to early robustness is the presence from the start of the design process of the manager of the future organization. Combined in these instances are ownership of the design and of the start-up requirements needed for future success. Secondly, the manager and his team, which implements the design, commit themselves to stay at least through the start-up period and into the early stage of steady state operation. Lastly, success and survival of alternative forms of organization particularly depend on leadership by mature, confident individuals who understand themselves and can accommodate a substantial amount of ambiguity. Such managers have only a slight dependence on rules and control mechanisms. Seen either as an advantage or a disadvantage, alternative forms of organization do require more competent managers than the great majority on the scene today.

Lastly, the search for enhancing the quality of working life has taken a number of directions. The most productive and longest lasting appear to be the new or alternative forms of organization. These will have profound effects on managements and unions stimulating a substantial rethinking of their structures and functions. Those unable, incapable, or afraid to undertake the rethinking will offer resistance that is likely to be considerable. Additionally, the roles of the leaders of these institutions, their related professionals, and the schools that prepare these people all face significant alteration.

REFERENCES

Albert Cherns. 1976. "The Principles of Sociotechnical Design." *Human Relations* 29.

Louis E. Davis. 1982. "Organization Design." In *Industrial Engineering Handbook,* edited by G. Salvendy, chap. 11-1.

Louis E. Davis. 1980a. "Individuals and the Organization." *California Management Review* 22, no. 2 (Spring):5–14.

Louis E. Davis. 1980b. "A Labour-Management Contract and Quality of Working Life." *Journal of Occupational Behavior* 1, no. 1:29.

Louis E. Davis. 1979. "Optimizing Organization—Plant Design." *Organizational Dynamics* (Autumn) 3.

Louis E. Davis. 1977. "Evolving Alternative Organization Designs: Their Sociotechnical Bases." *Human Relations* 3:261.

Louis E. Davis. 1971. "The Coming Crisis for Production Management." *International Journal of Production Research* 9, no. 1:65.

Fred E. Emery and Eric L. Trist. 1973. *Towards A Social Ecology.* New York: Plenum Press.

Fred E. Emery and Eric L. Trist. 1965. "Causal Texture of Organizational Environment." *Human Relations* 18:21–32.

C. Paul Hill. 1972. *Towards a New Philosophy of Management.* New York: Barnes & Noble Books.

Edward E. Lawler III. 1978. "The New Plant Revolution." *Organizational Dynamics* 3 (Winter).

Eric Miller. 1959. "Technology, Territory, Time." *Human Relations* 12, no. 3:243.

Richard T. Pascale and Anthony G. Athos. 1981. *The Art of Japanese Management.* New York: Simon and Schuster.

Donald A. Schon. 1971. *Beyond the Stable State.* London: Temple Smith; New York: W. W. Norton.

Sir Geoffrey Vickers. 1970. *Freedom in a Rocking Boat.* New York: Basic Books.

Daniel Yankelovich. 1981. *New Rules.* New York: Random House.

6
QWL – The State of the Art

Albert Cherns

The "art" in the title of this chapter is, like all art, socially located. It owes its origins and its development less to the imagination and inventiveness of its practitioners, though like all art it does that as well, than to the developments in the societies in which it has emerged. When our art began, changes in technology and in the social organization of work had simultaneously transformed our societies' potential for creating wealth and the relationship of man to machine in that process. We had entered the age of the complex organization whose power seemed excessive, whose impersonality rendered it faceless, and whose appetite for resources was gargantuan. Feared and hated, the organization was yet the bearer of the horn of plenty. Employing organizations have become not only the creators but the distributors of the material and moral resources of society: they provide incomes, pay taxes, and confer status and prestige. Our positions in society depend on our relationship to employment: organizations are the instruments of governments' social and economic policies, the state itself must serve as the instrument of organizations' policies providing and maintaining the infrastructure that they find essential.

Work organizations depend upon society and its institutions and they on them; between organizations and society there is an accommodation, part law, part custom, and part bargain, that regulates their relationship, defining what the organization can claim and what society can expect. Concern with the quality of working life (QWL) has developed at a time when that accommodation has been shifting and under question. Nobody needs reminding that the expenditure of nonrenewable resources is an issue of our time. Industry, and I do not wish to confine that word to manufacture but to use it as shorthand for work organizations (a very old meaning of industry is diligent work), is being required to become custodian and creator of society's resources rather than their user. In the hubbub over "natural" resources and pollution, the fact that society's resources are human as well as material may not always register. Nevertheless, the accommodation to which I referred includes rules and conventions, customs and expectations about how "socially responsible" industry uses the human resources of society.

Industry is today less free to choose whom it will hire, whom it will fire, the contractual terms on which it will employ, the conditions and safety of work, than it was in the not so distant past. And in Scandinavia we see the start of regulation of the nature of the work itself. How people are treated at work as well as their opportunity to have work is becoming the legitimate concern of governments. It is within the context of the changes in attitudes and values that this shift in accommodation represents that a growing number of organizations in many countries have been experimenting with new forms of organization of work. As ever, the few are ahead of their time, the many far behind.

I do not want to tell the story, interesting and suggestive though it is, of QWL from its beginnings in the British coal mines more than 30 years ago, through the Norwegian experiments of the late 1950s and 1960s, to the ferment of today with its unexpected focus in Canada. I *do* want to examine the context of QWL today and tomorrow because I am sure that what is happening now and will happen tomorrow are not mere extensions or extrapolations of the experiences of the last 20 years or even of the decade since the Arden House conference. The 1980s are no more like the 1970s than the 1970s resembled the 1960s; what was needed then, what worked then, will not necessarily work now. One very obvious difference is the composition of the supply of labor. The release of the married woman into employment continues to swell the supply at a time when the phenomenal ability of the last two decades to absorb the increase has disappeared. And the change in expectations, in education, and in values has been remarked and analyzed by so many that further mention is not required from me.

At the same time that the labor force, "the supply side" of the labor market, has been in a process of unprecedented change, the "demand side" has been extraordinarily turbulent. Industrialization in the developing countries has been accompanied by "deindustrialization" in the developed world. Manufacturing industry, which now employs fewer each year, employs fewer still of the unskilled. Moving from batch and mass production toward flow process, their need is for the new cognitive skills of information processing rather than the traditional industrial ones. Nor have we yet seen anything approaching the full consequences of the need to conserve energy. Any scenarios I could offer would be of no more interest or value than those of anyone else; I would merely make one point. The economies of scale that gave such clear advantage to the large organization are now in fairly even balance with the diseconomies; energy conservation in combination with the new information technologies, not to mention the problem of industrial relations, is shifting the advantage back toward the smaller unit.

Already the mismatch between supply and demand of labor is the source of great agony; unemployment has replaced inflation as the foremost problem of many countries. I may comment in passing that the failure to perceive the real nature and implications of this phenomenon may prove enormously costly; the concept of unemployment imports many false assumptions about what are the appropriate and normal functions of man and woman in society. The problem looks different when we locate it in the modes of distribution of entitlements in society or in the relative utilities of time spent in paid and in unpaid work.

But however it is regarded, it seems that we are in the midst of profound changes in the structure of working life and in the meaning of work in society; the relatively brief period when work could be equated with paid employment seems to be ending. It is worth remembering that our concern with the quality of working life first manifested itself during that period, albeit at a late date. An emergent phenomenon of a world of work in rapid change, the QWL approach itself is changing and must continue to change. Surfacing first in the extractive and manufacturing industries, identifying the assembly line as the epitome of all it wished to change, it coincided with an acceleration of the shift of employment out of primary and secondary industry and, within primary and secondary industry, out of "direct" labor. Responding with growing emphasis on work in tertiary and quaternary industries — in banks, insurance offices, in distribution, in hospitals, in government agencies — QWL has encountered an especially rich field in computerization. Almost all efforts so far have been undertaken within employing organizations, within the field of paid employment. Paid employment is, of course, not about to disappear. And so long as the unavailability of paid employment is perceived as an aberration, no fundamental change in our outlook or in our practice is called for. But if full-time paid employment ceases to be seen as the norm, the meaning of work will change; it will no longer be seen to be synonymous with paid employment. And when the meaning of work changes, so will the meaning of the quality of working life.

A decade and more ago the debate was joined as to whether work was still a central life interest in our societies, and whether an approach that was predicated upon work as a central life interest was appropriate or relevant to those for whom work, or more accurately paid employment, played a purely instrumental part.

A balance, none too easy, was struck. For those for whom work was a central life interest — a majority of white collar but possibly a minority of blue collar workers — maximizing the intrinsic interest of their work was manifestly good. For the rest the big question was whether the "spillover" or the "compensation" hypothesis was true. For those for whom dissatisfaction at work entailed poor quality of nonworking life (spillover), then again improving the content of work was to their benefit. For those who compensated for daily drudgery by rich nonwork experience the advantages were questionable. As data accumulated it seemed that on the whole a richer work life promoted a richer nonwork life. Room, however, would still have to be found for those for whom work would or could only be instrumental to their standard of living, but not its quality.

But can we now be sure that work in the form of organizational employment will or can be the central life interest of most people? It is rash to forecast and no less rash to project current trends. But few, other than those who govern us, believe that the future will repeat the full employment of the 1960s. The microprocessor, the robot, expensive fuel, and competition from cheap labor economies all press toward economy of labor, while the contraction of the child-bearing, child-rearing span combines with the shift in values it has engendered to raise women's participation rate. International competition renders make-work and other forms of concealed unemployment uneconomic. Only a little imagination is needed to realize that work in the form of employment is likely to occupy a less central position in society than it has since the establishment of the modern industrial state. Industry is thought of as the producer of wealth; what is equally important but perhaps less obvious is that it is its distributor. Along with other employing organizations, industry distributes the material and moral resources of society, pay and prestige, our entitlement to be treated as its paid up (in both senses) members. If, as many believe, the growth of the "hidden economy" is a harbinger of the flight from employment, if employment is to occupy a lesser proportion of our active lifetimes, does QWL become a brief episode of late industrialism?

In assessing the state of our art we must search deeply the lessons we are learning from its practice. The growth of industry and the development of a society reliant upon, and dominated by, organizations had isolated, privatized, and alienated the individual. And the more employed work occupied the center, the more was alienation from work a wedge between the individual and society. Insofar as QWL has helped to restore meaning to work, it has lain a plank in the bridge between the individual and society. One important lesson to be drawn is that whatever displaces employment as the hinge, the *mechanism* by which entitlements are distributed, must possess *intrinsic meaning* to the recipient. Whatever we have to do to establish our rights must also be worth doing for its own sake. What we have learned about how to reestablish meaning in work may yet prove to be the most important.

Work will still be needed, though we may come to value that which contributes to the quality of life more highly than that which contributes to the standard of living. But the question will still arise: how should it be done and how organized? Here again we have learned that the best organization is a work community; we do not know whether a work community can again be a community at work. But the challenge is to extend our understanding of the quality of organizational life to the quality of community life.

In our assessment of the state of the art in *The Quality of Working Life* (Davis and Cherns 1975), we argued that because we value organizational employment so highly we rated its demands above all others save those of our immediate families. Absence from work to attend a football match is considered irresponsible only because we rank the duty to the employer higher than the duty to the team we support. As we wrote then, "we could argue that our culture places what should be the community's responsibility — to get society's work done — on the individual, while placing what should be the individual's responsibility — to make himself available for other people who need him — on impersonal community organizations."

The sociotechnical approach to QWL has progressed through two channels and the link between them. By focusing on task systems it has emphasized the alternatives in technical systems design. By identifying the personal and social requirements of members it has directed us to the development of "mini-societies", of self-maintaining work groups. And the instruments of sociotechnical analysis have proved to have the power to expose the requirements for both. Most of us who have worked with this approach have observed that the implications for technical redesign have been more readily appreciated and worked with than those for the design of community, or mini-society. We have been brought to see, therefore, that the technical system is only for convenience to be regarded as separate, jointly optimizable with the social system. For the purpose of community design it has to be seen as the principal component of the social systems' goal attainment subsystem, a very privileged component because in it is invested a very high proportion of the capital — physical, financial, and emotional — of the whole system. Much of the system's available energy is devoted to its protection from the effects of external pressures and vagaries.

More efficient technical systems offer society the possibility of investing far less of its available resources of human time and energy in the attainment of its production goals. If indeed we then reorient our goals toward the maintenance of community, much of the technical system becomes part, not of the goal attainment, but of the adaptation subsystem — flexible, responsive, and protective of rather than productive of its principal goals. We would then be redressing the imbalance of responsibilities to which I referred earlier.

The demand on the sociotechnical approach would then fall more heavily on its less well developed tools, those concerned with building self-maintaining communities. The approach would need to be modified, but not drastically. The first requirement would be to identify the tasks that are essential to community maintenance (that is, an analysis of the goal attainment system) and the establishment of the necessary roles and role relationships. We can do that now with productive organizations, and indeed, the improvement of our social system building points in that direction. I am hopeful, therefore, that the lessons we have learned and the methods we have evolved will prove robust enough and flexible enough to tackle new and welcome demands.

In the preceding part of this chapter, I have been led into speculation about a distant, though not too distant, future. I should now return to what is immediately before us. We are all well aware of the shift out of manufacturing employment. What is somewhat less immediately obvious is the shift of employment within organizations, manufacturing or otherwise. Our systems analysis of organizations draws attention to three factors — inputs, outputs, and transformation processes. Whether we are considering primary, secondary, or tertiary industry, historically the bulk of employment was centered on the transformation processes. The roles of those who worked on those processes were buried deep within the organization. Indeed it all began with the coalminers! It is these that have been mechanized, automated, and computerized.

More and more of the roles of those employed today lie on the boundaries between organizations, or in the boundaries between organizations and the public. Two consequences follow. First, as we know, occupants of boundary roles are subject to stresses of a different nature from those in embedded roles. Secondly, from the point of view of QWL, the interfaces between organizations and between organizations and the public become critical foci of analysis and design. The technical sophistication of these interfaces has focused on computerization whose inflexibility is the cause of immense frustration to clients, customers, and staff alike. Before even more sophisticated systems are developed with their doubtless even more excruciating unforeseen consequences, the sociotechnical redesign of organizational interfaces should be urgently explored.

It is clear from so much that has been said and written that QWL has been shifting in focus (and will have to continue to shift) to keep in step with the changes in our societies since the 1950s when the sociotechnical approach got under way and since the late 1960s when QWL began to attract attention. Most obviously, attitudes toward and values about technology have been changing. The choice of technology has been moving from one that was virtually exclusively the concern of the organization to one that is the concern of the community. If we have been able to play a part in helping to select, and even more to modify, technology on behalf of the organization, we shall in future find the need to play a part in selecting and modifying technology on behalf of society. How society's concern with technology will be expressed is naturally enough a function of the society concerned and takes different forms in different societies. Most interesting is the role of law. Societies with a conservative common law tradition confine themselves to regulatory instruments that depend on clear and identifiable standards, whether of pollution, or of safety, or of work environments. Societies with a tradition of positive law have more freedom to state more general objectives and provide them with some form of legal sanction. This approach has been taken by Sweden and especially by Norway. In a particular way this illustrates an interesting sociological law, as applicable to organizations as to societies: *The forces and processes that make for change in society are the same as those that maintain them intact.*

Organizations, like societies, are in a state of dynamic, not static, equilibrium. If, when we work with our organizations, we feel we have an uphill task working against the dominant forces, it is we who may have failed to understand the way change takes place in that organization. Of course we encounter a structural problem. The pace of change is slow and erratic, constantly interrupted by random events and intrusions, while the expectation put upon us is of swift, monotonic progress. Personally, I have learned to welcome with relief the overt and outward expression of anxiety and resistance. These outward signs serve with time to mobilize the forces of change. Patience rather than panic is required from the practitioner. We have sometimes placed ourselves in an awkward position. As evidence of the need for, and ultimate triumph of, QWL we point to the value changes in society, the changing demographic scene, the trend toward a postindustrial, postmaterialist society. We indicate that we must be on the winning side; if it, too, is to win, the organization should join us. But all around is evidence that others are not. Our own analysis *must* tell us that the odds are really against us. Yet we search for specific explanations if we fail and assume the successes are the norm. We should be looking for the specific explanations where we succeed. How to recognize, understand, and tap the dynamic in organizations is, I believe, the least well developed of our skills and understanding.

In this I feel we have really had little help from Organizational Development (OD) whose paradigm of unfreezing–changing–refreezing seems to me to describe the microscopic rather than the macroscopic processes that condition them. At the macro level we encounter continuous movement in the struggles for power, prestige, and resources within the organization.

Nevertheless, the dominant form of QWL intervention (note the term intervention—itself a term of OD art) is a mixture of dilute sociotechnical analysis and principles with OD practice. Just as OD has acquired somewhat different forms in the United States and in Europe, so has the sociotechnical component. In Europe the impact both of structural analysis and of structural remedies has been greater. In Britain, for example, it just will not do to ignore the extent to which workshop behavior is an expression of working class cultural values and experience. It is, of course, all very well for our Marxist critics to confront us with the deep structural sources of alienation in our capitalist societies; they are opposed to our whole enterprise from the start. But it does not, therefore, behove us to ignore those roots nor to ignore the relevance of the many other efforts to improve working life, however unsociotechnical they may be. Flextime and its variants — "single status," consultative and communicative structures, representative systems, quality circles, and safety committees — serve in different ways to crisscross the power structure and hierarchy of the organization. Some strengthen, others weaken, the binding of workers to their roles. If, as we do, we prefer the latter, we should not lose sight of the concept of organization-in-dynamic-equilibrium. Contradictory processes are inevitable, even necessary. Schon's (1971) concept of "dynamic conservatism" is a useful one to help interpretation.

And, however deep the origins of alienation in society, and I would maintain that alientation is inseparable from the forces needed to create and maintain society, the chief dangers lie in those symptoms described as forms of alienation by Seeman and widely accepted. We can assess our QWL as counteralienation strategy by setting its processes against Seeman's list. I believe it comes out like this:

Forms of Alienation	QWL Outcomes
Meaninglessness	Knowledge, understanding of role and organization
Powerlessness	Competence, shared responsibility
Normlessness	Group and team norms
Isolation	Membership
Self-estrangement	Self-development

It is not an unimpressive list. If, as I suggested earlier, we are in the future to use our knowledge, skills, and ideas in the service of community development, this achievement looks promising.

In my I fear somewhat disjointed account of the state of the art, I should try to assess what we have learned about the management of organizations designed according to the principles of QWL. If you ask a manager of one such organization whether his job is easier, he will unfailingly assert the contrary. It is different, but not easier; and perhaps harder. You are kept on your toes all the time, and you cannot get away with the facile solution. It is a new way of life but by no means free of conflict. Indeed, there may appear to be more conflict because it is overt not hidden. Above all, it is constructive conflict. The experience is challenging and bracing. The contrast with more conventional management is a cause both for rejoicing and for anxiety. If support within the organization is not matched by support from without, and in the case of multiple organizations it often is not, the strain on the manager and the obstacle to his career may be insupportable. And if time and effort is required to mobilize that external support, who is to do it?

These problems are also encountered early in the process of developing QWL within organizations. We have evolved useful procedures for generating task forces to prepare QWL changes in key activities, departments, or units within the organization. They soon produce as by-products of their process of analysis some highly useful ideas that could solve immediate and long-standing problems without diverting them from their longer range concerns. Almost inevitably the task forces are met with defensive managerial responses, which they receive as indications that nothing has changed and nothing will change. They find it hard to accept that management will change slowly and uncertainly, here and there, not everywhere at once. Frustration is high and threatens to disintegrate the task force. Yet we cannot wait until all management has been convinced and has changed before we start. And we cannot hold task forces back from trying to have obvious nonsense put right. Engendering a tone of confidence and optimism without complacency is a tough number. Yet sooner or later most task forces begin to feel their muscle, and comparatively small successes act as a tonic. The shared feeling of fighting even though unsuccessfully brings the task force together.

One problem that worries many of us is the organization's predilection for "packages." It is natural to want to know outcomes in advance. It is equally understandable that managers are happier with something they can "take" and then leave if they feel like it. If QWL and the 80s conference is "what we had in 1981," it will not go far. Yet can we simply offer an open-ended commitment? If package we must, it is less harmful to package the process than the product, to offer a more or less standard way of involving people in projects of redesign than a standard solution in the form of semiautonomous work groups. By their workings, not by their works, shall ye know them!

I want to end by discussing outcomes. The literature is not short of "accredited outcomes"—lower absenteeism, better quality, improved productivity. These are encouraging and good for the shop window. They are, however, less important in the long term than the capacity to withstand stress, the flexibility to introduce new developments, and the ability to solve problems that are far less easily measured.

Organizations can be understood through their mythology. Much is expressed in catch phrases: "Don't ask me; I only work here"; and "Don't stand still or you'll be painted white," express the way people choose to perceive their relationship to the organization. It is far more important to understand people's belief systems than to measure their "job satisfaction." That is why we should be looking at their cognitive maps, their sense of personal competence, and their modes of conceptualizing the organization and their relationship to it. It is perhaps no exaggeration to say that our systems of measurement, both of organizational outcomes and of personal outcomes, have been unhelpful, if not positively antagonistic, to QWL.

Let me end with two stories that illustrate this point. At the invitation of a colleague who had been working with the organization, I accompanied him to a meeting that included the president of the corporation and his aides, and the chairman of the group within the organization with which my colleagues had been working and his acolytes. In the course of conversation the president remarked that, "we now know how to manage our 75s and our 100s and perhaps even our 350s, but our 700s and 1000s give us a headache." While understanding that he was referring to the number of people employed at each of the sites, I thought this a somewhat unusual mode of expression that nevertheless showed a clear understanding of the problems of management of human resources. Somewhat later in the discussion the president turned to the group chairman and said, "But you know, X, we at corporate level have to measure you by the dollars and cents." At this I demurred, saying, "When you spoke earlier you showed quite clearly that you perceive the most difficult environment of the organization to be the people-environment, yet now you turn to the man who is facing that environment on your behalf and tell him that although he is doing a good job in that respect, you cannot take it into account in the measures that you apply. Surely there is a contradiction here?" "No," he replied, "there is no contradiction. I don't think there is any contradiction . . . yet maybe I will have to think about it." So far as I know he is still thinking about it, though this was a few years ago. I have not been in touch with him since.

The second story concerns an organization that had a very advanced personnel management that made liberal use of job satisfaction questionnaires with feedback. The charts showed steadily improving scores in many departments. In one department, X, the changes had been quite dramatic up to the last questionnaire but one from which it was omitted. I asked what happened. "Well," came the reply, "shortly before the last round we opened a new department and asked for volunteers. Most of the volunteers came from Department X, so the membership of Department X was mostly too new to be given the questionnaires."

"Why did they leave?"

"They didn't want to work with the computer we planned to install in Department X."

Perhaps the questionnaire was on the right lines after all!

REFERENCES

Davis, L. E. and Cherns, A. B. 1975. *The Quality of Working Life: Volume I: Problems, Prospects and The State of the Art.* New York: Free Press.

7

International Perspectives on QWL

Einar Thorsrud

When white society, early in this century, found no more space on the maps into which it could expand, its perceptions of the world and of itself started to change. When it found that the old rules of the game between people and nations were no longer accepted in the manner to which it was accustomed, it started to panic. There were no fixed points in the environment any more that could tell white society where it was, who it was, and where it was going.

In the late 1920s and early 1930s, there were numerous artistic and literary accounts of white society and its inhabitants fumbling in the dark trying to find something to hold on to. Isherwood's novel, *I Am a Camera* (later made into the film, *Cabaret*), gives us a good picture of how humans behave when they feel that the ground they are standing on is slipping away.

There was at least one man who did not panic in that situation; his name was Hitler. He had the right kind of madness to fit the new world. One would have thought he taught us a lesson: that we should watch out when a leader of a powerful establishment is facing a turbulent situation and claims to possess the knowledge of exactly what needs to be done according to the *old rules of the game*. We should also watch out when someone comes up with *one single new set of rules* that will put everything right.

I shall not pursue this pessimistic perspective, but I shall look into my personal experience with quality of working life (QWL) on the international level and will go back to the early 1970s.

THE TURBULENT WORLD OF ORGANIZATIONS

The turbulent socioeconomic field was a basic issue at the first international conference on QWL at Arden House in 1972 (Davis and Cherns 1975).

97

Emery and Trist (1963) had already for nearly ten years been aware of the basic change in the nature of the environment where work is done. They had been forced to realize, through long-term change projects in the industry of countries as different as England and Norway, that the overall situation was changing, at least in two basic ways. First, that the *degree of interdependence* among forces causing change had increased to a new level. Second, *uncertainty* had also increased to make the environment appear quite confusing. The increased interdependence is clearly demonstrated in the economic crisis after the oil price shock in 1974. The increased uncertainty is clearly demonstrated by the microchip revolution—what could be a little gadget turns out to spark off something like an earthquake if we cannot place it in a proper context.

In the previous phase of development, the phase of mechanization culminating in the late 1950s and early 1960s, organizations could survive by accumulating larger and larger productive resources in big organizations competing with others on the basis of product and people specialization. This phase was over in the late 1960s.

Researchers who understood technology as well as social systems, like Donald Schon (1971), gave similar warnings as Emery and Trist. The industrialized countries had gone "beyond the stable state."

When the international QWL network met in 1972, we were only some 60 people, mostly academics who lived on the boundary between the university and working life. But we still had enough evidence from years of field work and systematic observation to draw some conclusions.

- When we put into international perspective a case like Lordstown, where the workers had started to revolt against the brand new, fully automated car factory, we were able to make a broadly based judgement about what it meant. It was not a single case of poor factory design or bad labor management; it was a strong and persistent warning from a new generation of workers that they were not going to put up with the old stick-and-carrot type of treatment. They wanted respect as human beings. They would choose unemployment compensation rather than becoming part of a monster machine.

- When we surveyed the state of the art in an international conference on QWL, we felt confident we could take on large-scale projects or programs, as long as we were willing and able to collaborate and support each other across national and professional boundaries. We could also see what we needed to do to improve our methods, theories, and strategies. We could plan cooperation to achieve this.

- By cooperating across national and professional boundaries, managers, union leaders, and researchers could feel that they had some common purpose and could do something that would, at least in their own local environments, reduce the uncertainties that might otherwise create infighting and other negative behavior. We could see enough of that in the academic world.

It is one thing for "observers"—researchers—to see the misfit between the organizations of yesterday and the turbulent environment of today and tomorrow. It is another thing for the major actors in the drama, industrial and trade union leaders, to experience that same misfit. How do they react?

Fifteen years ago the second field project (Hunsfos) in the Norwegian Industrial Democracy project had just started to take off. It was partly because of the new knowledge gained at Hunsfos that Emery and Trist could make Shell U.K. interested in trying to move in the same direction. Then it became important for both projects that a Shell group visit Hunsfos. The visiting group had to understand both the background (the Norwegian situation) and the object of change (the new factory organization). It was only then, when both the figure and the ground were understood, that the Shell people could see what it meant to do something similar in a different situation. For the Norwegians, it was only when they had to explain to outsiders both the national and local background and the new factory organization that they could see clearly the old and the new interdependencies, for example, how they had to establish new types of contracts with suppliers of raw materials as well as with the agents buying their products. They could also better see the new type of complexity they were dealing with, for example, the need to change the planning system, the maintenance, and gradually also their product mix when they changed the processing of pulp and paper. (Later some of the critical relations changed to a level far beyond the capacity of one single company to cope with.)

When the Shell group came to Oslo, the Norwegian trade union leaders explained how, under the Norwegian conditions, the unions could support the project on a local level. By explaining to outsiders, they became much more aware of what they were actually doing. And by defending their position, they became more committed to the basic ideas.

When people move across boundaries in this way, psychologically, professionally, and culturally, they have a unique chance to learn and change. They become aware of the new "maps of knowledge" that are open to them and the new value systems they can test out. They suddenly see their own world differently. An English plant manager remarked: "What this Norwegian shop steward says and does, is something I should have liked to see more of on the company boards I have to deal with." I remember well how the shop steward pulled me aside and said: "Why is it that I can never make my top union leaders see what we do here?" (What happened in this event was repeated during a later visit by an Irish group coming to Norway.)

What I have just described is more than simply stating that one can learn by traveling to another country. In fact, I have stated something about searching abroad to find concrete answers to important questions. I am also stressing that perhaps it is necessary to cross cultural borders to be free enough from national conventions and old "maps of knowledge" to learn something fundamentally new—which is what we have to do when we want to reorganize work for the future.

There are several lessons to be drawn from this when we take an international point of view on QWL. First, it is necessary to search wider than within national boundaries to find new knowledge and the right people with the necessary skills to use it. We had to go from Norway to England to find the researchers we needed. This applies not only to researchers whose main business should be new knowledge; it applies also to engineers and managers in a certain branch of industry. And it applies to trade union leaders.

The second lesson is that it is not only a matter of getting access to the new knowledge and skills. It is also a matter of checking the links abroad, links on which critical interdependencies are based. Intuitively we know that these interdependencies do not stop at the national border. And we would be better off if we went across the border to see what it will mean for the future if we move in this or that direction in a turbulent world. What we check across the border is mainly of an ethical nature, a matter of norms and values. Will we have a safety net, a social network to rely on, when we take the risk of moving into unknown territory, unknown ways of dealing with our unpredictable future?

Third, if we judge the possible consequences of important changes across the border, it means we have to become conscious of the criteria we use when we make critical judgements or evaluations. When we do that, and decide to act accordingly, we also find out on a very real basis not only who we are ourselves but also who our real friends and enemies are in the new environment. And let us not fool ourselves: there are very real confrontations out there in the process of change waiting for us. If we assume that others in the learning process such as managers, workers, and union leaders have to change their roles while we maintain our old role, then we— the scientists, the researchers, the specialists—continue to fit the world of yesterday. There are enough frustrated and alienated academic people around to show what this means. We have as researchers a special responsibility to record, analyze, and make available to others what we learn. The other partners in this basic learning process also have their special roles to fill. (So far, I have used the national boundary to illustrate the importance of learning in a different environment than one's own. In some countries, the regional differences are perhaps big enough to create the similar possibility of learning.)

The fourth lesson to be learned is that we, the researchers, should be careful not to fall into the trap and assume that *we* are basically helping *others* to learn. If that is what we think, we have missed the main lesson, namely that we can only learn when we join the other learners—when joint, shared learning takes place. This means that any type of basic change mechanisms that we happen to invest cannot be kept alive if we alone take ownership of them and include them in that special tool kit we carry around as researchers.

BASIC CHANGES IN AN INTERNATIONALLY INTEGRATED BRANCH

Let me now turn to a different type of international event, namely a form of search or participative planning meeting that may take place when a highly international industry like shipping faces a basically new type of environment. This was the case in 1967 when we had done our first pilot studies on board ships and when at least one company with some 30 ships in international trade was willing to share with us what they thought would be their future.

We arranged a seminar in Holland where two Norwegian, one English, and one Dutch shipping company met. Some representatives of unions, different public agencies, and research groups also took part to explore the past, present, and future of the sociotechnical design of ships. We also explored strategies of change to initiate participation in planning and collaborative development projects, rather than specialist-dominated projects. Without going into detail, I think the following lessons were learned:

- The specialists in ship design made sure there were no basic innovations in technology they did not know of that might drastically alter the trends they knew already. (For example, that the size of ships had reached its limit, and that no basically new propulsion system was anticipated.) By assuring themselves of all this, the technical specialists were better prepared to move into the unknown, and they felt they were partners in something important, not only competitors.
- Some representatives of unions and the school system gave some early warnings of what was coming and what critical role the schools and the unions would play in creating new training and new career patterns.
- The researchers felt assured that their experiences from other branches of industry were valid in shipping. They also felt the trust and respect of other professionals, and they were helped to understand some basic differences between industry ashore and what they faced in shipping.
- An international network was starting to develop not only between researchers but also between shipping people, and representatives of unions and public agencies. Jointly they were getting in better position to approach governmental and international agencies, international unions, and employers organizations.

Ten years later this 1967 meeting was repeated. This time evaluation of basic changes was undertaken jointly. The same agencies were involved but this time there were more companies present with seamen from different levels of the ships and shipping firms. One further lesson was learned during this event: the joint evaluation of similar projects opens up a kind of learning, not only of new solutions, but also of new strategies by which solutions can be reached and by which self-sustained learning can be sustained. This learning means that the real actors control diffusion.

INTERNATIONAL AGENCIES AND QWL

Let us also briefly reflect on a different type of international perspective on QWL, namely the role of international agencies like International Labor Organization (ILO), United Nations Development Program (UNDP), European Economic Community (EEC), Organization for Economic Cooperation and Development (OECD), and other international institutions involved in QWL. And let us not forget the international unions and employers agencies at a time when a new type of trade union, Solidarity in Poland, plays a very critical role in world affairs.

In 1974 the International Labor Organization in collaboration with a Norwegian governmental agency arranged an international seminar on industrial democracy. Tripartite groups and specialists from many countries took part. We could not avoid the ordinary plenary sessions, but there were also a number of group activities and field visits. After the conference different types of small special seminars or workshops took place in the mountains or in local community settings. These excursions were accepted mainly for touristic reasons, but they turned out to be something more than that. There are some lessons to be learned from this conference experience.

The negative experience of traditionally organized international conferences to disseminate new knowledge and experience was confirmed. Some information did get across in plenary sessions, but almost nothing that could not have been achieved better in other ways. Mostly the specialists talked to each other over the heads of the main actors in the field. Different political groupings assured themselves and others that their own system was the best.

Another lesson is that in the shadow of the official program, during meals and in the evenings, many small groups met informally and exchanged concrete experiences. By doing so they started to get a better overview of the world situation in QWL and the basic changes taking place.

A third lesson came from the small special seminars taking place in local settings. These seminars did influence a number of national and enterprise groups to learn from each other and to consider how to start something new at home.

A fourth lesson is that the professional specialists learned little or nothing from the plenary arrangements, but some of them learned from the small seminars in such a way that they were later engaged in collaborative projects in different countries. The trouble was that by doing this through the aid of international agencies their roles were forced back into the traditional bureaucratic hierarchy existing on the professional and international levels.

Development Projects under ILO

A somewhat unique type of international project emerged from the 1974 ILO conference simply because an international agency official realized that new forms of work organization could not be introduced through the normal ways and means of his agency (Kanawaty 1981). A very modest, open-end program was developed for Tanzania and India in direct collaboration between the two countries and a Norwegian research center. Without going into detail, at least a few basic lessons to be learned from these projects can be mentioned.

The projects had to be sealed off and protected both in the international agency and in national institutions to prevent them from being coopted and bureaucratized. (Even national projects run this risk. An example of that is the huge "Humanization of Work Programme" in West Germany [Pöhler 1979].)

Another lesson is that on the national level the selection of agencies to handle the projects could not be left entirely to the governments. Any outside involvement in this would be difficult if the project was financially significant. Anything big would be subject to competition between institutions and professionals while the nature of the project depended on cooperation across institutional and professional boundaries (Kanawaty and Thorsrud 1981).

A third lesson is that the major results of the project were not primarily specific knowledge about new forms of work organization in developing countries. That had been learned before by, for example, Nitish De, his colleagues, and several Indian enterprises. What was new was the particular type of open-ended, participative planning used to carry out the projects on the national and enterprise levels.

An important lesson was learned regarding the level of education necessary for participation in this kind of international project. Contrary to what is taken for granted, namely that a low level of general education is a serious constraint, we learned the opposite. Over-education particularly among technical and managerial staff is a major constraint because it tends to reinforce traditional, status-oriented forms of organization rather than task-oriented work systems. People with higher education try to move from where they are to something better, rather than to improve the work place where they are.

Still another lesson is that limited social science or other specialist competence among project staff members is not a basic problem if the staff becomes actively involved in project planning from the first minute — not only in their own country but preferably on an international level as well. If this occurs a very important network may develop, not only between the so-called developed and the developing countries, but more important, directly between the developing countries. A serious problem is the segmentation of professionals within public agencies and private and public enterprises. This segmentation can as easily be reinforced as it can be reduced through international projects (Thorsrud 1981).

A final lesson, which was a by-product of these small projects, was the effect they had on the agencies involved. The agency in India (National Productivity Council) has definitely changed its own approach to organizational change and QWL. It has also changed the content of material it uses for teaching enterprises and professionals what work organizations may be like in the future. This change in the content of information about QWL also occurred in ILO as an international agency (Kanawaty 1980). The projects also had an impact upon ILO's role as an information center with a new section dealing with QWL.

MULTINATIONAL CORPORATIONS AND QWL

We cannot conclude these rather personal reflections on QWL in an international perspective without mentioning the multinational corporations. Let me again be specific and use my own experience. It comes from the offshore oil industry in the North Sea.

In 1977 a search conference was set up, somewhat like the one in shipping ten years earlier. The shipping conference was easy in the sense that we were already accepted as a development partner by two powerful enterprises and at least one strong union. In the offshore industry, we faced four of the big oil companies of which two wanted to have as little as possible to do with unions, researchers, and governmental agencies. A Norwegian subsidiary of a big multinational corporation took a leading role, and since this enterprise and the government wanted our involvement, the other organizations followed. They could not afford not to particpate if they wanted to have a long-term involvement in a rapidly growing industry.

Since 1977 we have spent months and years on network building and preparatory studies. Now we have more opportunities for research than we can possibly manage — projects ranging from sociotechnical design of a platform worth as much as our annual defense budget to projects on offshore employment and its consequences for the family and local community. It is far too early to draw any conclusions, but some preliminary observations can be made (Qvale 1980).

The difference between the multinationals is very great indeed in terms of how they handle QWL issues. Some of them seemed to think Norway can be treated like a banana republic. On the other hand, some of them are as much aware of the needs for changes in QWL and are as willing and able to participate in change projects as the corresponding Norwegian companies. A few of the most short-term profit-oriented firms are already on their way out of the North Sea with a reputation that will gradually make it difficult for them to operate in similar development projects.

The government-enterprise-union interaction, which in this case is absolutely essential, is equally difficult for all three parties for two main reasons. One is the well-known bureaucratic syndrome. The other is less well known, namely that all three parties need policy initiatives from the "center up" in their own organization. Even more they need the ability to work out policies and practices through some sort of matrix across bureaucratic and organizational boundaries. Some such mechanisms have already been created, and some of them help to establish some degree of control over economic activities. Others, more concretely, help to control safety, job security, educational, and labor-management practices. Much remains to be done in this area.

The enormous size of investments and cash flow, the combination of old and new technology, and the hundreds of organizations interacting to design, build, and operate platforms is a good example of what big business is going to look like in the future. One experience from the North Sea oil industry is that the centralized control of specialized units used now by private firms and governmental agencies does not work. The design projects in which we are involved are not only sociotechnical; they include complex institutional redesign. In this process I think we can neither accept the multinationals as they are nor can we overlook the fact that they may, at least some of them, have considerable potential for changing more quickly and in a more adequate way than some of the other actors in this big game. One thing the multinationals can do to prove that they are seriously adapting to a new type of future is to demonstrate that they accept that profit is only one of the criteria of success. Another form of proof will be collaboration with governmental agencies in responsible utilization of natural resources. A third proof would be to accept the shared responsibility of enterprises for their impact on local communities and particularly on employment.

QWL AND THE INTERNATIONAL EMPLOYMENT CRISIS

From the point of view of QWL, I am afraid we do not have as much of a contribution to make to the solution of the growing mass unemployment as we should. However, some members of the QWL network have made an effort to show that the problem is not one that can be solved quickly. What we are faced with is a worldwide depression, not just a little dip in the growth curve that we had begun to believe could last forever (Emery 1978). Others have shown that unemployment cannot be solved on national levels, nor only among the rich world nations (De 1981).

Many of us are aware of, and have contributed in our own small way, to the need to stimulate many small experiments to create new employment, particularly among youth. But I do not know of anyone who has produced a strategy comprehensive enough to deal with the main problem. What we have seen so far from governments and international agencies is mostly based on the assumption that the growth we experienced up to the mid-1970s can be resumed. This is not a realistic assumption if we accept the massive amount of evidence that we are actually faced with the "collapse of work" (Jenkins and Sherman 1979)—when work is defined in the traditional way.

Even in countries where some economic growth can be expected, we are faced with at least three sectors of the labor market between which a major reshuffle needs to take place:

- One privileged sector where people have *jobs* (paid employment) *and work* to do.
- A second sector where there are *jobs but little work* left to do.
- A third sector where there are few or *no jobs but plenty of work* to do (in homes and voluntary service).

I can see no realistic way of solving the employment problem just by increasing the number of jobs in the first, privileged sector.

With this massive problem in front of us, I will end this chapter outlining my very incomplete and rather personal view of QWL in an international perspective. We need not despair if we go on from here with a sense of value and conscious that we move in the same direction. But if we stop here, scared stiff of the perspectives we are faced with—if we do nothing but to describe a coming disaster—we are in fact contributing to it.

REFERENCES

Davis, L. E., and Cherns, A. B. 1975. *The Quality of Working Life*. New York and London: Free Press.

De, N. 1981. "A Perspective on Global Policy Planning for Development." Draft document for the Conference on QWL and the 1980s, Toronto, August 1981.

Emery, F. E. 1978. *The Fifth Wave*. Canberra: Centre for Continuing Education.

Emery, F. E., and Trist, E. L. 1963. "The Causal Texture of Organizational Environment." (Reprinted in *Human Relations* 18, 1965).

Jenkins, C., and Sherman, B. 1979. *The Collapse of Work*. London: Eyre Methuen.

Kanawaty, G., ed. 1980. *Managing and Developing New Forms of Work Organization*. Geneva: International Labour Organisation.

Kanawaty, G., and Thorsrud, E. 1981. "Field Experiences with New Forms of Work Organization." *International Labour Review* 120, no. 3.

Pöhler, W. 1979. *Damit die Arbict menschlicher wird*. Bonn: Nerlag Neue Gesellschaft.

Qvale, T. U. 1980. "Socio-technical Design of Offshore Work Organizations." Oslo: Work Research Institute.

Schon, D. 1971. *Beyond the Stable State*. New York: Basic Books.

Thorsrud, E. 1981, with Semiono J., and Singh, J. P. "The I.L.O.—NORAD Project on New Forms of Work Organization in India and Tanzania." Geneva: International Labour Organisation.

8
Sociotechnical Foundations for a New Social Order

Fred Emery

> The myth of the machine and the cult of divine kingship rose together.
> Lewis Mumford, *The Myth of the Machine.*

There are reasons to believe that the world economy is once again in the throes of a phase change. There are also reasons to believe that this phase change, like the preceding ones, will involve a paradigmatic shift in the organization of people around their work. If this is so, then our perceptions of what has happened in the past decade or more in the world of work may need to be modified: likewise our perceptions of where those changes are leading us.

I do not wish to dwell on the first proposition but will have to comment on it in order to give sufficient reason for us to take seriously the second proposition about "the paradigmatic shift."

It was only in early 1978 that I was alerted to the possibility that the Kondratieff hypothesis might have to be taken seriously. Since G. Garry's critique in 1943, I had regarded that hypothesis as "unproven." Since about 1950 I fully accepted the economists' claim that Keynes had advanced their science to the point that only governmental mismanagement could precipitate another depression, and the Bretton Woods Agreements would enable any such outbreak to be confined to the mismanaged nation.

It has not been difficult to establish that Garry was wrong. Kondratieff's historical statistical series were certainly incomplete and inconclusive, but the trends he detected were fully validated by our analysis of the comprehensive series of historical statistics that were now available (Banks 1971; Mitchell 1971). Blainey and Singer and Small's historical studies of gold discoveries and of wars (Blainey 1970, 1973; Singer and Small 1972) had disposed of Garry's argument that "even if the K-cycles of activity/depression in the world economy did occur they were explainable in terms of the *exogenous* factors of gold discoveries and wars; hence they did not indicate any inherent and predictably recurrent instability in the world economic system." Garry seized upon one further weakness in Kondratieff's position, namely that he had not suggested a dynamic that might explain how the international system could generate such serious instabilities at approximately 50-year intervals. So long as this elaboration was absent the Kondratieff hypothesis had doubtful scientific status; one did not know whether it belonged to metereology, economics, or psycho-cultural cycles.

The Massachusetts Institute of Technology computer simulation of a national economy has resolved this last problem in Kondratieff's favor (Forrester 1976). Our national economies run in a way that naturally generates the K-cycles. I might note in passing that the centrally-planned economies have the same fundamental difficulty in correlating the production of consumer and producer goods. On the historical facts, the political revolution of 1917 did nothing to protect the Union of Soviet Socialist Republics from the 1930s depression and is doing nothing for the Soviet Bloc members now.

Granted the scientific status of the Kondratieff hypothesis, there is still the practical question. Is the depression now on us, is this just another business cycle with the depression likely in the late 1980s; or is Walt Rostow (1978) right in his amazing suggestion that we went into the depression in late 1972 and are now on another long upswing? The facts only permit one of the first two answers. There could be some sort of brief recovery as in 1976–78, but that is unlikely to restore the so-called propensity to invest or effective demand.

I have come this far down this line of discussion because I think there is a relation between these developments and the seriousness with which employers pursue quality of working life (QWL). I will go further to suggest that in periods of growth employers will toy with QWL in order to accommodate to cultural changes, and temporarily suspend such games during a downturn in the business cycle. However, in struggling to get out of a prolonged depression they will not be just playing. Let me now go back to pick up the path leading to the second proposition presented in my opening remarks — that these depressions are phase changes in the world system involving the ruling paradigm of work.

I concluded, in 1979, that the Kondratieff hypothesis had to be taken seriously (for the reasons given above). It seemed obvious that each of the depression periods, the 1830–40s, 1880–90s, and the late 1920s and the 1930s, should be studied for clues as to the nature and effects of this class of system crises. No national statistical series were available to me that would pinpoint the economic crisis of around 1790, and hence that critical period in modern history was left as a shadowy thing relative to the interpretation of the other periods. (Phyllis Deane, in the second, 1978, edition of her *The First Industrial Revolution* has presented statistical evidence that Britain suffered a deep economic depression in the 1780s and also in the 1740s, pp. 109–11, particularly Figure 1.)

Certain common features readily emerge. The emergence of the world economy (circa 1780) and its regular breakdown at long intervals introduced a new element into social life. Prosperity, change, and continual improvement in the conditions of life come to be seen as the normal way of things. After a generation and more of this the proof of the social system does indeed appear to be in the eating.

The onset of a great depression is inevitably seen against such an historical background of progress. The social system that has come to be taken for granted by the general populace itself becomes the object of attention and questioning as their expectations are dashed. The questioning is all the more critical because the economic setback does not at all seem like the result of crop failures, or the hand of God. What a depression challenges is not just a mass of individual expectations but a socially dominant world view that has given sanction to many of the central institutions of the society and to their relations of mutual support or condescension.

It is this that makes every great depression a *potential* producer of social revolution. Close study of modern revolutions has led scholars to arrive at the same conclusion:

> Revolutions are most likely to occur when a prolonged period of objective economic and social development is followed by a short period of sharp reversal. The all-important effect on the minds of people in a particular society is to produce, during the former period, an expectation of a continued ability to satisfy needs — which continue to rise — and during the latter, a mental state of anxiety and frustration when manifest reality breaks away from anticipated reality. The actual state of socio-economic development is less significant than the expectation that past progress, now blocked, can and must continue in the future. . . . The crucial factor is the vague or specific fear that ground gained over a long period of time will be quickly lost. [Davies 1962, pp. 6–7]

Before the emergence of the world economy the persistence of poverty and the frequent recurrence of starvation due to crop failures and wars did not bring about social revolution. At most the sporadic uprisings confirmed that there was no alternative to the existing order but disorder, pillaging, and brigandage. At best the hope was for some justice within the traditional order, not a reordering that might free people from their traditional roles.

The social instability induced by the long waves in the world economy can be observed in each of the great depressions. The potential for social revolution is, however, as much manifested by counterrevolution as by revolutionary action. The potential is far more widely manifested in the ferment of revolutionary ideas that appears to affect all areas of human endeavor in these periods and have passionate sway over the masses of people, not just the intelligentsia whose business it is to trade in ideas.

The ideas that come to have such a sway on popular thinking do not usually emerge in the period of economic crisis itself. Typically they have gained intellectual currency in the period of economic slowdown before the depression. This makes it easier to discern which of the many ideas in this preceding period of intellectual (not social) ferment are likely to take a hold. Similarly, the institutional changes that are closely tied to these new ideas are as likely as not to appear in the last days before the economic depression as in the period of depression. So in this respect also there should be some clues.

Some implications seem clear from the past history of depression periods. Thus we would expect that the onset of a great depression in the 1980s will change the tempo and direction of the trends observed in the 1950s and 1960s:

- greater tension in the work force and in industrial relations;
- predatory behavior amongst corporations (corporate cannibalism);
- shrinkage of governmental budgets;
- renewed social polarization of haves and have-nots;
- *popular* challenge to the prevailing institutional myths about governance, the economy, religion, education, family, and human ideals;
- a reversal of the movement to liberalize trade between nations (increasing autarky).

In short, all of the contracts between people, their neighbors, their masters, and their gods are likely to be called into question.

Each *recovery* from economic depression also had certain common economic technical features. Each time recovery was marked by:

- the adoption, on a large scale, of *new technologies* that created new markets and greatly enhanced investment possibilities (Schumpeter 1939);
- the adoption of new forms of distribution to serve wider and more scattered markets (Emery 1967);
- the emergence of new forms of energy that were cheaper, simpler to exploit, and more flexible (from water power, to coal, to electricity, to oil, to gas);
- a step-wise expansion of sources of raw materials and labor (for example, the opening of the prairies and tropical plantations and the great waves of internal and international migration);
- emergence of new forms of business organization (Aglietta 1979).

It was some time before I realized that there was in all of this a critical integrating factor. It was apparently not enough for new investments and new corporate forms to bring together new technologies, new forms of energy, and new supplies of labor. New forms of labor organization appeared. Nor, apparently, was it enough for each management and plant to find its own best solution. At each crisis a generalized solution appears to have emerged. Each time it was as if a new generation of labor was being subjected to a new form of industrial discipline.

Let us examine those statements. The first phase of industrialization did not emerge on the back of any particular technological revolution and certainly not on the back of the steam engine. Tunzelbaum (1978) has amply documented the fact that the steam engine and steam driven machines only became a significant factor in the textile industry of Britain in the recovery from the depression of 1830–40s.

The industrial system emerged on the basis of the "factory system," a form of work organization, *not* a new technology. At the heart of the factory system were the following features:

- the centralization of work places "under a single roof" — the physical definition of a factory;
- the fencing in of the factory and imposition of control over access or departure at the factory gate;
- the imposition of a strict working day and working week;
- the allocation, where possible, of fixed geographical work posts;
- a detailed division of labor that enhanced the role of semiskilled workers at the expense of the multi-skilled craftsmen;
- the creation of a class of unskilled labor to enable the semiskilled operatives to devote themselves to their allotted tasks and provide a reserve force against daily fluctuations in attendance. In the cottage craft system the only unskilled were those in formal or informal apprenticeship;
- the creation of a class of workers whose established and exclusive function is the supervision of the work of others — the foremen.

Within the factories no one person produces a marketable product; he or she contributes to just a part or facet. This laboring at details does not equip them to enter any commodity markets as private producer. None of these essential features of the early system of manufacturing rests on the introduction of more efficient technologies, although hand tools went through a very rapid evolution to fit the requirements of specialized detail laborers.

The governing principle of the system of manufacture was *the subjective division of labor* within a master-servant relation. It contrasted markedly with the putting-out system. The putting-out system was still basically a free market in which cottage craftsmen negotiated the value they added to the merchants' material through the equipment and labor they had at their own disposal. It was a relation of symmetrical dependence, not the asymmetrical dependence of a master-servant relation. The efficiency of cottage-based production rested on the flexibility of multi-skilling not on division of labor.

With the wisdom of hindsight we can see that the economic viability of the early system of manufacturing did not arise from greater productive efficiency. It certainly increased the rate of circulation of the merchants' capital and reduced transport costs, but it did not get more output from the same labor inputs. It was more *effective* in getting more work out of people and hence more production. It was able to do this because, for the relatively free market of the putting-out system, they were able to substitute the very unfree labor market of that era. That labor market was unorganized, except for the minority of key craftsmen and their apprentices.

It was also a market in which there were no customs, norms, and traditions such as gave the servant some rights in the more personalized asymmetrical dependency of feudalism; and no legislative controls other than the existing criminal and property laws. The cottage craftsmen were under the constraints of community and kin to maintain some standards of civilized existence. The manufacturers were under no such constraint (Marcus 1974). It is little wonder that the cottage craftsmen, for the most part, preferred to slowly starve to death rather than submit themselves or their family members to the tyranny and indignity of factory employment. It is little wonder either that they attributed their difficulties, first and foremost, to unfair competition arising from the unfree labor market of dispossessed people. Despite the myth that has arisen, the prime object of the Luddite movement was the undercutting manufacturer not the newfangled machines. Breaking up the machines had much the same significance as the traditional burning of the wicked landowners hay ricks — striking at the hip-pocket nerve. In the first instance the manufacturer's capital was rendered unproductive until the machines were replaced, a lengthy process in those days, and in the latter instance the landowner was disabled from carrying stock through the winter.

Andrew Ure, who was writing at a time much closer to those events, was in no two minds about what was the central integrating feature of emergent industrialism. We remember Richard Arkwright as the inventor of the spinning frame. Maybe he just stole the idea for his invention as he subsequently stole so many other ideas, but Ure could see that:

> The main difficulty ... lay ... above all in training human beings to renounce their desultory habits of work, and to identify themselves with the unvarying regularity of the complex automation. To devise and administer a successful code of factory discipline, suited to the necessities of factory diligence, was the Herculean endeavour, the noble (sic) achievement of Arkwright! Even at the present day ... it is found nearly impossible to convert persons past the age of puberty, into useful factory hands. [quoted by Marx 1906, vol. 1, p. 463]

The principles of factory discipline had to be learned again when the Lowells founded the textile industry of New England (Kasson 1977).

I have dwelt on this first phase of industrialism because it so clearly illustrates the central integrating role of principles of work organization. The early factory system of organization made it possible to adopt and successfully exploit existing inventions such as Arkwright's spinning frame and the over-shot water wheel; inventions that quite likely would not have found a role in the putting-out system. The factory system did not emerge just because those technologies existed, contrary to Schumpeter's thesis (1939). We can see also that this first phase of industrialism provided a fertile seed bed for the technological developments that were to be so eagerly seized upon in the next phase, *after* a new principle of work organization had appeared.

The transition to the second phase of industrialism is important to our understanding of industrialism. It is important because we have tended to fuse the first and second phases and see the factory system as the natural consequence of the invention of steam driven machinery. The machinery available at the emergence of the second phase offered a great increase in efficiency, provided it could be powered by steam and located near sources of coal. This combination would have to provide an irresistible reason for centralizing labor in factories. It is such a rational explanation that we assume that is what happened. Such is our myth of the birth of industrialism; and it remains a potent and persistent source of distortion in our attempts to understand what is happening in industry today. We even persist in using the term manufacturing when it properly relates to only the first phase before the emergence of machinofacture.

The second phase emerges with the acceptance of an organizing principle that underlies all succeeding phases, at least until now. This is what Marx called the *objective* division of labor. The factory adopted machines to further reduce dependence on the small but critical group of craftsmen and to achieve the efficiencies that steam-powered machinery was beginning to demonstrate. With this development it no longer made sense to allocate people to work with those tools and tasks for which they were subjectively best fitted. People had to be allocated to whatever tasks were needed to keep the machines producing. These tasks were dictated by the design of the particular machines but general classes of jobs emerged, for example, the attendants who watched the machine for signs of malfunctioning, the feeders and off-loaders, the sweepers, the oilers and greasers, the maintenance mechanics, the millwrights, the boilermen, the shifters, and the storemen.

This constitutes a very significant step in "the regression of the product." Under subjective division of labor the product moves out of reach of its producer to a commodity market he cannot enter as a producer-seller. However, the detail laborer still contributes something of the product itself even if it is only stitching a collar to the shirt. With machinofacture he is simply feeding and maintaining the beast; the beast takes the raw materials and makes the product. This is a figure-ground reversal. In manufacture the worker dictated what his tools did, and apparently he contributed greatly to the design and evolution of those tools. In machinofacture the machine dictated what the worker did; and factory workers contributed very little to machine design.

In reviewing this transition it might appear that, although we had misjudged the nature of the first phase of industrialism, here at last were the real beginnings of industrial society. At least, we might argue, from about the 1840s technology came into dominance and began to dictate the pace of growth and the forms of industrial organization. Certainly the growth of industrial civilization between the world economic crisis of the 1830s and 1840s and the next great crisis of 1880s and early 1890s was like nothing that could be recalled. The great industrial exhibitions of London and Paris in the 1850s were paeans of praise for the revolution wrought by the dominance of technology in this first age of machinofacture. Haeckel and many many others were preaching a new religion — scientific materialism. God was irrelevant and the day of doom put off forever as the marriage of science, technology, and industry guaranteed a prospect of boundless progress. Looking back it is easy to understand and forgive this short-sighted ebullience.

Of more significance in understanding how that second phase of industrialism continues to color our present thinking is the fact that two such incompatible social philosophers as Max Weber and Frederick Engels arrived at this same conclusion, despite the "great depression" of the 1880s and early 1890s. Max Weber foresaw the bureaucratization of all walks of society, because this was the rational and predictable way of achieving efficiency in the allocation of resources to create reward. Frederick Engels put it more eloquently, in terms that read like the Old Testament:

> If man by dint of his knowledge and inventive genius, has subdued the forces of nature, the latter avenge themselves upon him by subjecting him, insofar as he employs them, to a veritable despotism *independent of all social organization.* [Engels 1894]

It was Lewis Mumford who so succinctly labeled this as the "myth of the machine." He thus identified a prime case of misplaced concreteness.

Machinofacture emerged from the womb of manufacturing. Machines were being designed for the factory market not for the poverty stricken and nearly defunct cottage industries. Industry was dividing into the now traditional departments of producer goods and consumer goods, and the "foolproof" machine was coming into its own. The point is this: insofar as technology after the 1840s appeared to set the pace for economic growth and dictate the forms of industrial organization it did so only on the basis of the assumptions already established within the system of manufacturing. It completed the process of getting the craftsman out of the direct processes of production (not, however, out of the tool room and boiler room or out of maintenance).

Now let us stand back from the details of the first and second phases of industrialism. Taking a broader historical perspective we notice that these earlier phases were of only academic interest so long as we, in the 1970s and 1980s, thought that we were now confronted with the emergence of just another phase in the series. When it appeared that we might possibly be confronted with a *system change*, not just a phase change, a reconsideration of these early periods became imperative. Such reconsideration became imperative because it was necessary to identify the principles governing the *whole* system of industrialism through all of its phases, not just the specific principles governing the phase we are in and the phase from which ours immediately arose.

In *Futures We Are In* (Emery 1977), I thought it sufficient to tackle the latter task. I tried to spell out the paradigm of scientific management that Frederick Taylor devised to lead the way out of the economic crisis of the 1880s and 1890s. I also tried to spell out the paradigm of the assembly line; the paradigm that has dominated the post-1930s depression phase. I do not think it is difficult to deduce from that book what I thought would happen next in industrial organization. I clearly believed that a new paradigm of work was emerging and hence, at least, a new phase of industrialism. I do not think that I rated the change higher than that. My expectation was that the general adoption of the principle of "self-managing production groups" (semiautonomous groups) would domesticate industrialism and promote changes in nonwork areas.

Within this new paradigm the foreman and the unskilled laborer would start to disappear and the worker would gain the dignity of himself deciding what to do and deciding what was meaningful work. At the same time, the product was tending to recede further as computer tape-instructed machines, microprocessors, diagnosed faults and physical sensors replaced human attendants. Self-managing groups and quality control circles reverse this tendency. As groups they can map a production line and identify something that is *their* product.

Kumar (1978) and Aglietta (1979) have recently confirmed what Marx and, 130 years later, von Tunzelbaum had asserted. Recovery from the deep crises of industrialism has always depended upon the emergence of a more effective *social* form for eliciting productivity. No technology was sufficient in itself to create such a growth in productivity. At this point in time we have to consider whether the new paradigm of work is just a reaction to the increase in automation of productive activities. Certainly, we find once again that the leadership in adopting the new paradigm of work comes from those that stand to gain most from the new technologies. But, yet once again, the widespread adoption of the technologies follows from and does not precede and determine the organization of work. It is within the context of self-managing work groups and quality control circles that major corporations are seeking the adoption of new technology (*Business Week*, May 11, 1981). In such a context technological change is significantly less threatening to workers (Emery and Thorsrud 1976).

I think I have been wrong in thinking that all that will happen this time will be a replay of Schumpeter's scenario—a massive shift of capital into a new branch of industry. If that were so then it is easy to identify the microprocessor as the steam engine of the next phase of growth (Emery 1977). Aglietta's arguments (1979, pp. 385–86) have convinced me that the critical growth must come from achieving greatly increased productivity in the infrastructure areas of health, education, and welfare. This growth will come from opening these fields to private enterprise, as is implicit in the welfare scheme of guaranteed minimum incomes, and the widespread replacement of those bureaucracies by democratization of their work places in hospitals, schools, prisons, and the like. In this setting consumerism will sprout new wings.

The last four paradigms of work can each be identified as members of a series. They all presuppose asymmetrical dependence and the correlative sanctity of managerial prerogatives. The generative principle of the series was that of maximizing the proportion of the working day that each worker actually spent on working. With the assembly line, the last excuse for taking a bit of a break from the job was eliminated; there was no longer any excuse for walking away to pick up something. Note, however, that the currently emerging paradigm is a break with that series. It presupposes relations that are more nearly those of symmetrical dependence as the production goals and membership of the self-managing groups become the subject of negotiation and the concept of managerial prerogatives becomes secularized. The generative principle is no longer that of screwing out a high proportion of labor time from the working day. Efficiency of production is the generative principle for both work groups and managers. In this context the individual worker regains some time of his own during the shift and an ability to pursue some purposes of his own. It is not quite as good as getting time off for golf, but it is a reversal of a 200-year trend that ended only with Lordstown in 1972.

This new paradigm does not fit into the historical series that I have outlined. It would have to constitute a system change, not just a phase change in the old system. A system change in the nature of the wage relation could not stop short of a massive change in the social infrastructure creating the next generations of workers.

EMERGING CHARACTERISTICS OF A NEW SOCIAL ORDER

With each of the phase changes in the sociotechnical basis of industrial civilization we have seen something of the massive changes required in the associated social infrastructure. It has taken the wide-sweeping minds of people like Siegfried Giedion (1948), Lewis Mumford (1967), R. J. Forbes (1971), and Carlo Cipolla (1962) to reveal this to us. Because of the work of such people we have some sense of the great waves of migration, urbanism, secular education, artistic innovation, scientific discovery, and so forth that have periodically convulsed industrial society. Now that we seem to be confronted with a system change and not just a phase change we must be prepared to confront even more radical convulsions.

There are any number of threads that one might pick up to trace out how our social infrastructure might evolve. I have chosen to pick up the educational thread. Education is the thread that became dominant in the motif woven by the last phase of industrialism and, in these last years of crisis, has become "the whipping boy" for the collapse of personal and social expectations.

If this is the beginning of the end of the master-servant relationship, then what do we do with an education that has, since compulsory, secular education emerged in the 1880s and 1890s, educated young people to serve in the master-servant relationship? If industry and its administrative systems have had to move toward a self-governing paradigm of symmetrical dependence rather than asymmetrical dependence, then for whom are the educational institutions producing the old product? Producing people for mature industries and civil services locked into the backwaters of tradition must fail and cause dependent clients to similarily fail. Those industries are, of course, extremely vociferous in defense of their conservatism. Typically, they are the industries that find most comfort in avoiding change and are most able to get tariff protection by joining employers' federations, chambers of commerce, and the like. It is second nature to them to get governments to provide them with what they need—including the kind of employees they need. The big powerful corporations in the science-based industries do not typically work through those bodies. They are, however, the pace setters in employee practices. They are the ones the educationists must watch. The modern trend in education toward producing more independent and emotionally mature students would seem to be in keeping with the advanced personnel practices of the modern corporations.

At the same time the greater emphasis on education on the job calls into question the massive investment we have made in tertiary education. The excessive division of labor that justified the mass production of experts has had its day. The tertiary degree will have about the same relevance to economic recovery as the V-8 car engine.

On the basis of the matters I have discussed I cannot see how we can recover to take up the economic growth path we were on in the 1960s, nor can I see any hope of reestablishing autocracy as the norm of employment. If recovery is not likely to conform to tradition, if we are to think along new lines, then we must try and see what are the most probable strands that will interweave to give us some sort of new system.

The major reason for the system change is a shift in values in the community profound enough to be referred to as a cultural revolution, rather than any shortage of resources. This effect has spread into the work place and makes it impossible to recover productivity in the way that we did before. We cannot get the productivity out of our workers or managers in the traditional manner, not even with microprocessing. I have identified what I think are five salient strands, four of which would be on anyone's collection of starters. They are arranged in Figure 8.1 in an order that depicts the extremes: on the one side the pressure for a low energy, high equity society and, on the other, the pressure for a high technology society.

I am not alone in thinking a low-energy, more equitable society to be a very probable future for Australia. Recently the Sentry Insurance Company commissioned Professor Roger Layton and his wife, from the University of New South Wales, to do a survey of the Australian work force. In that 1978 survey, alternative scenarios of the future were put to people asking them which they thought was *most probable* and what they thought *most desirable*. About one-third of the sample of Australian workers, trade union leaders, managers, and public administrators, when asked about the *most*

FIGURE 8.1.

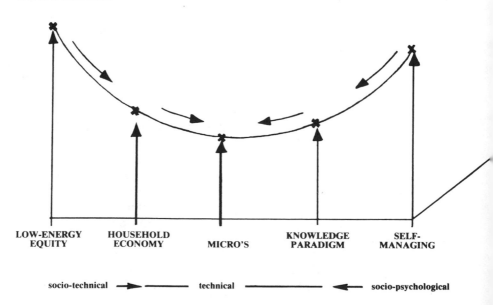

probable futures, replied that they could not see past a continuing depression scenario. Of the two-thirds who could see past a depression scenario, half saw a normal recovery to a 1960 type society of high-energy usage and inevitable social inequity (although few thought it "most desirable"). The other half, however, reckoned that the most probable future was "small-is-beautiful" : "low energy" and "social equity." I was very surprised at this finding because I thought that this scenario would be known only to tertiary-educated people and middle class trendies. The mass media in Australia had given this scenario no serious attention so we have to assume that people had worked this out for themselves.

One can, of course, ask one question beyond that: even if people think that the "small-is-beautiful" scenario is the most probable future, do they understand enough about the way the economy works? Are they being realistic? There is an answer, given by a group in Argentina who modeled the major regions of the world economy in order to see what changes would have to take place to enable South America, Central America, South East Asia, India and Australasia to provide for the basic needs of their people in the year 2000 (Herrara 1976). When they modeled these economies they tested the implications of two different optimization criteria. One was the classical capitalist system, where resources are allocated so as to maximize growth in the Gross Domestic Product (G.D.P.). The other criterion was the allocation of resources so as to maximize the average life span of the population. They inferred, for a number of reasons, that optimizing to increase the average life span of a population was the best way to ensuring movement toward a more equitable society. The first criterion corresponds to Layton's high-energy, social-inequity scenario and the second to his low-energy, social-equity scenario.

The question was then posed as to what growth rates would be needed under these different conditions to eliminate poverty by the year 2000. On their figures Australia would need to average a growth rate of 15 percent per annum to achieve this goal if resources were allocated in the usual fashion. The Australian economy has never sustained anything like this rate of growth for any past stretch of 20 years. I have already noted that even a 3 percent growth rate has had to be discarded as over optimistic (Emery 1978). We must also note that there are nowhere in sight the energy resources that would be needed to fuel such growth rates. By comparison this target of no poverty in year 2000 would be achieved by an average 2 percent growth rate if resources were allocated on the criteria of maximizing average life span. Put that way, the low-energy, high-equity scenario does not seem anywhere nearly as unrealistic as attempting to recover along the 1960s path of high-energy, low-equity.

I can keep my comments brief on two of the threads presented in Figure 8.1. The microprocessor revolution has been widely discussed, and we are beginning to realize that it is not just another technological step forward in the long series from water-powered looms and steam driven hammers. In conjunction with electronic sensors and "chip memories" the microprocessor will inevitably revolutionize the interface between man and machines, man and knowledge. The vast hordes of workers pouring in and out of mass assembly plants, department stores, and huge office blocks will become a thing of the past. Equally, the long, lifetime commitment to a job will also disappear. We have adjusted to this sort of problem in the past by formally recognizing all sorts of claims on the national wealth other than engaging in paid employment (for example, pensions, scholarships, fellowships, long service leave).

Gershuny (1978) and Scott Burns (1975) have pointed to a related phenomenon: the rapid growth of various forms of self-employment and pursuit of ways of reducing dependence on salaried wages. The evidence they have adduced suggests that this is no passing fad. It is a trend, furthermore, that should be considerably strengthened by the spread of the microprocessors into household equipment. As with Singers' new sewing machine, the microprocessor overcomes skill barriers that previously gave home-produced products a bad name.

Just as I earlier suggested that the human energy crisis has been more critical for industry than the fuel crisis so now I am going a step further to suggest that *the knowledge revolution may be in the release of human capabilities rather than in microprocessors, optic fibres, and satellites.*

SURPASSING THE TRADITIONAL BARRIER BETWEEN INTELLECTUAL AND MANUAL LABOR

The massive growth of higher education and science-based technologies has served only to reinforce the historical antithesis between intellectual and manual labor. In a seminal monograph, Alfred Sohn-Rethel (1978) has spelled out in detail how profound and persistent is that antithesis. It emerged with Plato's philosophy, Euclid's geometry, and Aristotle's formal logic. These unique, unprecedented, and unparalleled concatenations of intellectual explosions all took place in the fourth century B.C. and, to all intents and purposes, rose in one tiny geographical spot, the grove of Academus, one mile northwest of Athens. It is said that when Plato opened his think-tank there in 387 B.C., he inscribed over the entrance, "Let no man ignorant of geometry enter here." In that one brief historical moment intellectual labor proved that it could create a product incommensurably superior to any product of manual labor or the senses. They had produced truths that were timeless and universal. No such intellectual explosion occurred in any other culture, and nothing like it was to be seen until the seventeenth century in Europe. In that century the potential uniqueness of the product of intellectual labor was reasserted in the theoretical inventions of Galileo, Cartesian geometry, and Newton. The precarious claims that the Aristotleans had for producing a unique and superior intellectual product by logical induction from the observed facts were gradually surpassed by the claims of science. After Einstein there was no doubt about what were the strongest grounds for defending the claim of the uniqueness of the product of intellectual labor. Those grounds were in science, not in law and theology.

If we are going to gain an understanding of the antithesis between intellectual and manual labor then we have to understand the nature of intellectual labor. No one, I suggest, is going to understand the nature of intellectual labor until they grasp what was done by Euclid, Galileo, Newton, and Einstein. Nor will they understand the sacrifices that modern societies will undergo while they wait for another such genius. All the rest—the technicians, technologists, and scientists—are but the army of ants who labor in vain if the queen ant does not turn up. The unique intellectual product cannot be produced by educating people in the sciences or any other body of scholarly knowledge. The facts are against any such idea. In each of the cases mentioned above there was a step forward in timeless, universal theory. Each step forward was a great step toward the understanding and control of natural forces. Each step was also a miracle. They were miracles because there was no apparent way in which these great advances in systematic theory could have emerged from just seeing something that others had not noticed, for example, an apple falling on their head. They could not have arisen in the way that a recipe is discovered by a very perceptive cook or in the way that Edison contributed so much to our technical know-how. The theoretical advances we are talking about could only be the work of human geniuses: although that explanation tells us nothing about how to invent theory.

The division we observe today between scientists and technologists, the experts, and the ordinary workers at bench and desk is located quite precisely in the historical events that I have outlined. This division is first and foremost a division between those who can, alone or through their community, trace the logical proof of their ideas back to the great systemic structures erected by Euclid, Newton, Einstein, and so forth, and those who cannot. Years of tertiary education are seen as necessary before a person can be expected to be able to logically relate, through his disciplinary community, its textbooks, handbooks, and professional journals, to these unquestionable systemic foundations. More than that, the "science of psychology" postulates that only a few people have the innate ability to grasp these systemic concepts. Piaget's scheme of the physiological maturation of human intellect ends with the achievement of "propositional operations" at adolescence. Very few people mature to the point where they can grasp the higher levels of abstraction. It was said, perhaps for effect, that at any one time there were only four or five people who really understood Einstein's theory of relativity. The implication was clear: intellectual knowledge had become so esoteric that there could be no question of participative management of that knowledge. And this was not trivial knowledge; it was the knowledge that built the bomb and offered the solution to energy shortages.

The few who can grasp and work with such "fourth order" concepts are at the peak of academic excellence and constitute the high priests of the scientific and technical establishments. The nearest parallel in the field of manual labor would be the inventors, and they rarely command social respect or support.

In the process of democratizing work we have not squarely confronted this historical division of intellectual and manual labor. The removal of the foreman and first line supervisors only affected the source of know-how not the locus of expert knowledge. Democratizing the work place has certainly created greater openness at the boundary between expert and operative personnel but the polarity persists. It persists even when direct forms of participation in departmental management have been devised for example the "jury" system (Emery 1981). In a sense all of the forms of participation in management decision making must seem somewhat suspect when the experts employed by management constitute a special source of authority.

This is not just a theoretical possibility. Quite early in the Norwegian Industrial Democracy Program we identified two "black belts" of resistance to democratization. We were already very familiar with one. Beyond the reach of trade union agreements and the power of trade union officials there was a whole defense system based on local custom and usage and assuming that any management-inspired change had to be a change for the worse. The second black belt had not been foreseen, or at least had only appeared as a shade of grey. We had thought of the engineers, chemical technologists, and the like as simply part of middle management who would fall in line with the wishes of top management. We had not anticipated the extent to which they would feel threatened by the release of knowledge to the shop floor and had not realized the extent to which these experts had their own managers "binded with science."

The "deep slice" technique of participative design (Emery and Emery 1976) was a partial answer to this source of resistance. At least it gave the experts a chance to negotiate directly with operatives about their new boundaries. Beyond that I blithely thought that this problem of "Red and Expert," as Mao Tse-tung had phrased it, would be resolved by democratization of the educational process in the tertiary educational institutions.

Having now been over a draft of Trevor Williams's new book (1982), I think I have been glossing over a much deeper historical conflict between education and democracy. It is not simply a matter of debureaucratizing universities. My earlier confidence had come from a number of educational experiments that I had carried out in universities in the postwar decade. Compared with traditional programs it seemed well proven that *most* people benefited from controlling their own learning and their use of resources, including the negotiation of staff time and efforts. These experiments never ran more than three years, never involved more than one class at a time, and all included a good porportion of mature ex-servicemen. I was not particularly concerned that some students did not take kindly to such democratization, even though these exceptions included scholarly material that eventually made the professorial ranks. Equally, I was little concerned that these experiments were aborted as soon as I moved on. This seemed to be the usual preliminary reactions to new ideas.

The experiments reported by Trevor Williams have for me effectively reversed the figure-ground relation. He reports on experiments with undergraduate and postgraduate courses in management that have gone on under his control for the greater part of the 1970s. He reports also on a massive in-house educational program with the managers and technologists of Telecommunication Australia. On the surface the results are simply a repeat of what I and many others have demonstrated, that is, that *most* people do obviously benefit from the democratization of their learning. But this time there was a difference. Williams' work was on a scale that could not be ignored by the parent institution and he stayed around long enough to "cop the flak." There was one other matter contributing to the reversal of my perceptual field. I had been very closely involved with Trevor Williams in the designing and redesigning of his experiments without realizing that any radical shift in meaning was involved. However, with Merrelyn Emery I had been intensively engaged in studying the future of communications technologies and had been forced by the evidence to conclusions that converged on those arising from Trevor Williams' work. In the older technologies of the telephone exchange and the architecture of main-frame computers, it was sufficient to identify the way that designers had, without thinking, followed the same design principle as that embedded in bureaucratic organizations — reliability through building in redundant parts (Emery 1967). In the newer technologies involving the electronic handling of visual information, we were finding that the most fundamental assumptions were ones that concerned not these organizational alternatives but epistemological assumptions about the sheer physiological ability of people to gain information from the world around them. Wilbur Schramm, the international salesman for Education Tele-Vision for some two decades, has once again demonstrated that there is a fundamental mismatch between what television should be able to do, on those epistemological assumptions, and what it actually achieves (Schramm et al. 1960).

What Williams has done, in an eminently practical and constructive way, is to show us that as the outer layer of bureaucratic assumptions is peeled away the underlying assumptions about the incompetence of people to learn from their experience are evoked. As these deeper assumptions are evoked, the achievements of democratization are first challenged and then *destroyed or encapsulated.* Such a process of encapsulation was observed in Norway in the 1970s after the successes of the 1960s. Historically the negating processes have been found after most radical and popular revolutions (Marcuse 1966). In this case I think that destruction is not in the cards because there is no other way that offers comparable growth in productivity. Encapsulation is in the cards. Quality of working life could become a management tool that creates an elite of multi-skilled highly rewarded employees against a backdrop of large-scale unemployment and a multitude of short-term, part-time jobs in service industries. Note, however, that an encapsulation that preserves some of the critical managerial prerogatives within the corporation still does not seal off the enriching effects on the community of such multi-skilled, self-respecting workers.

The major service that Williams has done for us is to identify the fact that democratization of an area as significant as work cannot evade encapsulation unless the educational process is radically changed. This is not a new problem, but then I, and I guess many others, have not been looking back at the history of leaps and tumbles whereby we got to the spectacular period of growth in the years 1955–72. In what follows I want to use Williams' work as a vehicle to identify what I think are the emerging challenges in the process of democratizing work. I find that there is now little that is scientifically challenging in confronting autocracy in the work place. I find that there is a great deal in confronting the "meritocracy."

It would appear that whenever industrial society is in one of its recurrent periods of economic downturn and social turmoil, as in the 1960s, the relationship of education and democracy becomes a leading question. Thus, in the birth pangs of industrial civilization, Jean Jacques Rousseau gave us *Emile,* a plea for the humanization of education that would enable us to return to a true democracy based on peasant economy and craft industry. Moved by the terrible years of the 1830s and "the hungry forties," John Stuart Mills again asserted the intimate interdependence of education and democracy; that participative democracy required an educated citizenry but the requisite education could be gained only by participating in the governance of one's own affairs. Out of the "great depression" of the 1880s and the 1890s came Dewey with New Education; an education that was not to be simply a preparation for subsequent life in a democratic society but an apprenticeship in democratic living. In the economic, social, *and* political turmoil following World War I, G. D. H. Cole revived the broader emphases of Rousseau and Mills. The common core of these repeated attempts to introduce an alternative to the ruling paradigm of "representative democracy" has been identified by Carole Pateman:

The major function of participation in the theory of participative democracy is therefore an educative one, educative in the very widest sense, including both the psychological aspect and the gaining of practice in democratic skills and procedures. Thus there is no special problem about the stability of a participatory system; it is self-sustaining through the educative impact of the participatory process. [Pateman 1970, p. 42]

It is not surprising that this theme should arise in democratic societies when people's expectations have been crushed by economic disasters or world wars. Our faith in democratic forms of government is premised on the belief that the people know enough to contribute to their own governance. When the process of governance is failing to cope with economic and social change there will be those who see this as proof that we must go back to "rule by the few." There will be others, like Dewey, Cole, and Williams, who argue that what is called for are radical improvements in the ways in which people can know better what they want and have better ways of transforming that knowledge into control over their own affairs.

These are the two sides of the same penny. By the mid-nineteenth century it was clear to Mills that more education would not be transformed into more control in a *representative* democracy. The requisite education could be gained only by directly participating in formulating and making the decisions by which one is to be governed. This can be made to seem a ridiculous proposition by proposing such a question as: how can the *vox populi* meaningfully participate in deciding between defense expenditure on supersonic interceptor aircraft or aircraft carriers?

In the tradition of Dewey and Cole, Williams has directed our attention to the prior and more fundamental question for our times: how do we stop creating dumb-oxen, of even our middle management, and create a general confidence in an ability to learn from personal perceptions? If there is such a general ability, and people become confident in their possession of this ability, we can safely leave to the future the question of whether they can meaningfully participate in esoteric decisions about defense equipment. (Advances toward ways of participating in the higher order social decisions have already been made [Beer 1981].) In keeping with the relatively nonideological character of our times, Williams concentrated on the pragmatic (not the *idea* of pragmatism) to show what can be done in practice. As he ranged across the individual, organizational, and community levels, and two continents, it became obvious that the notion of "learning to learn" is central to any attempt to revitalize democracy.

Williams has clearly spelled out the further implication that revitalization of democracy must entail debureaucratization of our administrative structures, public and private. Beyond this he has stressed the need for a social change strategy that is very different from the top-down expert demonstrations that I was recommending in the hostile, unbelieving social climate of the early 1960s. I agree with this. It does in fact seem that the problem of de-bureaucratizing our societies is so huge that it can be accomplished only by a people who are confident in the validity of their own perceptions. The prevailing lack of faith in the experts is matched only by the lack of faith in elected representatives. But, at this point there is a very big **but**. By covering his experiences with democratizing work situations, management education, and university education, Williams has disclosed, in the strongest form I have yet encountered, a persistent, and the so far prevailing, lack of faith among people in the validity of their own perceptions.

Throughout his experiments Williams dutifully noted the university students, managers, and others who responded negatively to the learning opportunities with which they were presented. Among the managers were those who were upset because there was not enough structured exposure to and drilling in the existent body of management theory. As far as I can gather that criticism has not decreased since the end of the last series of workshops that he reports. Neither has the success of the university experiments over many years brought about any decline in criticisms.

This phenomenon is a common observation. For a great many years I thought it was probably a manifestation of what Erich Fromm termed "the fear of freedom"—something that was learned from growing up in an authoritarian climate and hence would be unlearned with experience of successfully managing one's own activities. For the latter learning to take place, we needed, I thought, only that the strong should carry the work through the initial learning phase. From the time we did the follow up study at the Hunsfoss Pulp and Paper Mill in 1967, I was uneasy and could not regard this hypothesis as other than just the best we had at the time. That follow up indicated that some of the opposition to the democratization of the work was coming from very competent *workers* who dismissed the evidence of their eyes and insisted that the improved performance of their more lowly colleagues was a consequence of their increased motivation and had nothing to do with their brains. As far as they were concerned it was only a matter of time before the Hunsfoss plant would have to recognize the intellectual incompetence of its general run of workers and promote *them*, the clever ones, to the level of foreman.

The work that Williams has done has brought us to where we are going beyond the point of simply challenging a traditional paradigm of organization. We effectively won that challenge by proving over and over again that better work could be done by groups that deposed first-line supervisors and managed their own productive activities. The role of the expert was relatively untouched by these developments. It seemed that self-managing groups of workers were as dependent on the experts as were the foreman. To go any further in the direction of self-management of one's own affairs it has become necessary to ask why the knowledge of the experts is so much more valuable than the knowledge that workers derive from performing their tasks.

When managers are given a chance to learn from their own experience and complain that they have thereby been deprived of real learning we have to reckon that we are up against something more than the paradigms of organization. I hesitated to suggest that we are hereby brought up against a more fundamental paradigm than that which is confronted by the democratization of work. Nevertheless, I am inclined to think that we are.

It seemed that we were getting to the fundamentals when Douglas MacGregor proposed his Theory X and Theory Y. Over the following years there was dispute about whether Theory Y could be achieved through individual job enrichment or autonomous work groups. That dispute has been more or less settled in favor of the latter. We are still saddled with the Williams problem: distrust of the expert, but no way out of dependency on those experts. This dilemma cannot be cracked unless we go beyond the challenge of the organizational paradigm to challenge the educational paradigm. It is education that sifts out and trains the expert.

It is not possible to challenge the prevailing educational paradigm by challenging the autocratic forms of delivering education. The problem is deeper than that. The only challenge that could possibly unseat the traditional paradigm of education is one that challenges the epistemology they take for granted. All of the education that results in a certificate of learning, in the capitalist or socialist world, is designed to overcome the "fact" that all human beings are basically incompetent to learn from any learning situation. They are basically incompetent because they do not possess the sensory organisms that would be needed to extract information from those potential learning situations.

It seems strange that the species that is the peak achievement of adaptive survival should be found to be fundamentally incompetent in learning about its environment. Strange, but that is precisely what was established by the British empiricists, Locke, Berkeley, and Hume at the birth of industrialism. Their immediate successor Kant did not refute this case but established that we gained even less from direct personal perception than they allowed. These gentlemen established the unchallengeable proposition that in the world described by Newton and Euclid, personal experience was limited to a kaleidoscopic inflow of sensations. In this inflow there is no direct evidence of the primary qualities of the things and events out there; no sensation can be seen to be determining any other; no ordering of sensations in space or time is directly perceivable. We can only infer these features from the shaky evidence of past associations.

Confronting this magisterial judgement was the fact that despite this formidable natural barrier mankind had attained such peaks of knowledge as represented by Newton, Euclid, Copernicus, Aristotle, and Aquinas. Much of this was the inexplicable product of genius, but there was also the long cumulative development of Aristotlean logic and the massive upsurge of the sciences in the seventeenth century. This latter experience suggested how man might deliberately plan to advance knowledge. The weak, partial, and fallible experience of the individual might be surpassed by a collective process of recording and accumulating observations; shifting, comparing, and classifying individual percepts to yield concepts and hierarchies of conceptual structures; purifying these by analysis, scholarly judgement, and the experimental testing of logical implications. This was the work of committed scholars and scientists and only those who were suitably trained and certified had access to the bodies of specialized knowledge that were thus accumulated. Note that "true knowledge" existed only in these accumulated stocks. Even the contributions of genius were unacceptable, unless they could be seen as additions to these stocks. This knowledge was *not* an accumulation of common sense, aphorisms, and folk sayings but stood in actively hostile competition.

From these understandings Herbart, who took over Kant's chair at Konigsberg, created the bases for all modern education. He showed that by controlled exposure, assiduous drilling, and carefully planned exercises, associations could be formed in the mind of a pupil that would approximate to parts of the conceptual structures established by scholarship. A so-called science of pedagogy was born to meet the emergency needs of industrial societies for mass education. The same principles carried over into the twentieth century expansion of secondary and tertiary education, Training Within Industry (T.W.I.), adult education, and management education. New audio-visual technologies were assimilated to the old paradigm that had produced the classroom, curricula, textbooks, chalk-and-talk, stick and carrot, and certificates of implantation.

When Einstein demonstrated that the universe was not in accord with the world of Newton and Euclid, people like Dewey and A.N. Whitehead began to question whether human experience was as barren and fallible as deducted by the Empiricists. These attacks on the dominant educational paradigm foundered on the demonstration that while Einstein had conquered the universe, the world of everyday objects and events to all intents and purposes still belonged to Newton and Euclid. Civil engineers and architects did not have to develop an Einsteinian mechanics, dynamics, or statics. The strong international movement for learning from experience (the New Education Fellowship) shrank into the box containing the only experience allowable as information in the Lockean paradigm — experience of one's own sensations and feelings as evidence of *subjective* states and changes. As embodied in recent fads for experiential learning and T-grouping they constitute no challenge to the traditional educational program. Managers exposed to experiential learning are thereby no less in need of chalk-and-talk about well-established conceptual models of the *objective world*.

What Newton and Euclid set up Heider and Gibson have now knocked down (Emery 1981). They succeeded in demonstrating that while the space-time of activity may be Euclidean the space-time of perception, and hence cognition, is *non*-Euclidean (Heider 1959; Gibson 1966, 1980). Veritable mountains of scientific data have been accumulated on how organisms perceive in a Euclidean world without doing more than perplexing us further as to how they ever managed to learn, adapt, and hence survive. By dropping the assumption of a Euclidean world Heider and Gibson have been able to show that human beings are marvelously well adapted to learn from their individual experience of the real non-Euclidean world. The world for each newborn member of the species is no "buzzing booming confusion" but a world for which they are predesigned by the successful evolution of their species, to extract survival-relevant information. And this they in fact do whether it is for finding the teat, avoiding cliffs when they start to crawl, or picking up the native tongue of their parents. By the same token they are at a loss when confronted by technological extensions of their senses, for example, television, based on the assumption that the perceptual systems have evolved to cope with a Euclidean world (Emery and Emery 1976).

With these findings the arguments of the Empiricists and Kant are demolished. While this might seem to be a matter of concern only for epistemologists, it is far from the case. This has destroyed the hitherto unchallengeable justification for the traditional educational paradigm. That paradigm is not intellectually bankrupt and logically indispensible. This is "checkmate"; not Dewey's call of "mate."

These discoveries confront us with a knowledge revolution whose implications far surpass the information revolution of the microprocessor. They challenge the very roots of Western literature civilization, as epitomized in Plato's parable of the Cave. In particular, and of concern to us here, these discoveries transform our traditional notion of expertise. In the traditional paradigm the true expert could only be one who had undertaken the years of detached study necessary to absorb knowledge from the accumulated stock of his discipline. Anyone else who claimed such knowledge was a charlatan or, remotely possible, a genius.

Within the new paradigm everyone is expert to some degree from the moment their experiences allow them some direct perception of the invariants in the environment with which they were interacting. They would be less expert to the degree that they had been trained to just look at the "facts" (*not* their inter-relatedness) and to the extent that they were inexperienced in looking. *In this new paradigm, knowledge emerges as the individual per-*

ceives the world. When two individuals share and reconcile their perceptions of the world, the process of accumulating social wisdom has already begun.

In the old paradigm these two individuals could not be held to make any contribution to knowledge unless they had both made reports about matters of fact, which they had not consulted about, to a trained inquirer, for example, the difficulty science had in accepting the existence of meteorites and "fire-ball" lightning. Even then such observations would not necessarily constitute a contribution to knowledge; it is only raw material. Only when it has been literally taken away and processed by a knowledge factory would we know whether it was "added value."

This contrast is brought into focus by the concept of a "search conference" (Emery and Emery 1978). I designed this kind of learning setting because, having left school at 14 years of age, I could not deny the learned authority with which men extracted lumber from forests, coal from mines, and wheat from fields (and women extracted meals from ovens), with no more than their shared experiences to go by. Even so I would not have ventured on this course without the moral support of such outstanding intellectual contemporaries as Heider, Asch, and Chein. They asserted, with considerable intellectual force, that if something was wrong it was in our basic assumptions about human nature, not in the obvious ability of individuals to learn, and learn to learn from each other. I was more than pleased by the outcomes of the search conferences we conducted in the late 1950s and the early 1960s. With the revival of the concept of the search conference in Australia, Norway, and the United States in the 1970s, there was a backlash. The backlash was straight from the old educational paradigm and it charged that: the search conferences were so designed that they excluded, or at least downplayed, the expert. The participants were therefore restricted to playing around with unprocessed facts. Given the illusion that they were engaged in accumulating knowledge they were in fact exposed to manipulation by conference managers who had equipped themselves beforehand with the processed facts.

Once the Heider-Gibson discoveries are understood, the search conference can be seen as a natural extension of the individual's power to explore and perceive how the world about him is structured and functioning. The real expert is then the one who has openly and widely experienced that particular world. The certified expert of the old educational paradigm is one who has that world, and his knowledge of it, classified into compartments and organized around issues that serve the aggrandisement of his discipline, not such mundane purposes as living in the particular world with which a search conference is concerned. The certificates of these experts are seriously deflated in value when people realize that they are themselves knowledgeable.

For more than 2000 years Western civilization has been haunted by Piato's description of the ordinary human state of knowledge as being that of observing shadows in a cave. This picture of the human lot was profoundly reinforced by Locke and others in the birth stage of industrial civilization. As peasant people were forced into wage dependence to power the industrial revolution, they pressed for democratic forms of government, if only to control the limits to their exploitation and their expected span of life. They managed to achieve the vote and representative forms of democracy. They were then led to believe that the shortcomings of representative democracy would be overcome when scholarships and free tertiary education enabled their sons and daughters to qualify as experts. This also was achieved. At this point, historically, we come to the point that Williams discovered in his studies — institutionalized education was itself now the major block to further democratization of society. I do not think that John Stuart Mill, John Dewey, or G. D. H. Cole could have conceived of such a fiendish contretemps in the affairs of people. I do not think that they could have predicted, for one moment, that educational institutions in the 1980s could have taken over the role of the church in Aquinas' century, the thirteenth century.

What Williams reports is not a replay of history, a recycling of elites. Institutionalized education has lost its claim to be the sole authority to certify experts — there are other ways to do that. Accepting that people can learn about the world "out there" from their individual perceptions, we can no longer find any intrinsic antinomy between democracy and education, between intellectual and manual labor.

When the common people "invent" theories about their world in their naively realistic way, they are engaged in the same kind of theory making as the scientists, ". . . fundamentally both can be regarded as limiting cases of one overall process, of a generalized kind of perception, in which no absolute knowledge is to be encountered" (Bohm 1965, p. 230). As the common people regain confidence in their ability to know the world, and gain the opportunities for knowing that open up with participative forms of self-government, we can expect a "knowledge revolution" that will rather overshadow the information revolution of the microprocessor.

CONCLUSION

The newly emerging paradigm of work is a clear break with the traditional factory system. The further development of this paradigm needs to be sought in the context of technological and sociocultural changes that are without precedent. It would be misleading to view the new paradigm as simply extending the factory system and yet further increasing the "recession of product from the producer."

The challenge is to work out the implications for the new paradigm of work that arise from the recent demise of the rationale for the historical division between manual and intellectual labor. If common sense and science are "fundamentally . . . limiting cases of one overall process, of a generalized kind of perception" then the historical barriers between work, management, and governance crumble. The barriers here are psychocultural, not sociotechnical.

The concept of sociotechnical systems has been, since Adam Smith and Marx, a very useful way of comprehending the evolution of industrial civilization. It could be a source of error in trying to comprehend emerging postindustrial systems that are essentially psychosocial (Emery 1970). In particular it could blind us to the persisting forms of the cult of divine rights.

REFERENCES

Aglietta, M. 1979. A Theory of Capitalist Regulation: The US Experience. New York: National Labor Board.

Banks, A. S. 1971. Cross-polity Time-series Data. Cambridge, Mass.: M.I.T. Press.

Beer, S. 1981. "On Heaping Our Science Together." In Systems Thinking, ed. F. E. Emery, vol. 2. London: Penguin.

Blainey, G. 1970. "A Theory of Mineral Discoveries." Economic History Review 23: 298–313.

Blainey, G. 1973. The Causes of War. London: Macmillan.

Bohm, D. 1963. Problems in the Basic Concepts of Physics. London: Dillons.

Bohm, D. 1965. The Special Theory of Relativity. New York: W. A. Benjamin.

Burns, S. 1975. Home Inc. Garden City, N.Y.: Doubleday.

Business Week. 1981. "The New Industrial Relations." Special report, May 11.

Cipolla, C. 1962. The Economic History of World Population. Harmondsworth: Penguin.

Davies, J. C. 1962. "Toward a theory of revolution." American Sociological Review 27: 6–7.

Deane, P. 1978. The First Industrial Revolution. 2nd ed. Cambridge University Press.

Emery, F. E. 1967. "The Next Thirty Years, Concepts, Methods and Anticipations." *Human Relations* 20:199–237.

Emery, F. E. 1970. *Freedom and Justice within Walls*. London: Tavistock Publications.

———. 1977. *Futures We Are In*. Leiden: Martinus Nijhoff.

———. 1978. "The fifth wave." In *Limits to Choice*, ed. F. E. Emery. Canberra: Australian National University, Centre For Continuing Education.

———. 1981. "Educational Paradigms." *Human Futures* (Spring).

———. 1981. "Adaptive Systems for Our Future Governance." In *Systems Thinking*, ed. F. E. Emery, vol. 2. 1962 ed. London: Penguin.

Emery, F. E., and Thorsrud, E. 1976. *Democracy at Work*. Leiden: Martinus Nijhoff.

Emery, F. E., and Emery, M. 1976. Appendix in F. E. Emery and E. Thorsrud 1976. Ibid.

Emery, F. E., and Emery, M. 1976. *A Choice of Futures*. Leiden: Martinus Nijhoff.

Emery, F. E., and Emery, M. 1978. "Searching." *Management Handbook for Public Administrators*. J. Sutherland: Van Nostrand.

Engels, F. 1894. "On Authority." In vol. 1 *Selected Works*, 1962 ed. Moscow: Foreign Languages Publishing House.

Forbes, R. J. 1971. *The Conquest of Nature*. Harmondsworth: Penguin.

Forrester, J. W. 1976. "Business Structure, Economic Cycles and National Policy." *Futures* (June).

Garry, G. 1943. "Kondratiev's Theory of Long Cycles." *Review Economic Statistics* 23: 203–20.

Gershuny, F. 1978. *After Industrial Society?* London: MacMillan Jordon.

Gibson, J. J. 1966. *The Senses Considered as Perceptual Systems*. Boston: Houghton Mifflin.

Gibson, J. J. 1980. *The Ecological Approach to Visual Perception*. Boston: Houghton Mifflin.

Giedion, S. 1948. *Mechanization Takes Command*. New York: Oxford University Press.

Heider, F. 1959. *On Perception and Event Structure and the Psychological Environment*. New York: International University Press.

Herrara, A. D. 1976. *Catastrophe or New Society*. Toronto: Institute for International Development.

Kasson, J. F. 1977. *Technology and Republican Values in America 1776–1900*. Harmondsworth: Penguin.

Kondratiev, M. D. 1935. "The Long Waves in Economic Life." *Review Economic Statistics* 17:105–15.

Kumar, K. 1978. *Prophecy and progress*. Harmondsworth: Penguin.

Layton, R. 1979. *What Then of the Future?* Australian Bulletin of Labour Development, 5,2.

MacGregor, Douglas. 1960. *The Human Side of the Enterprise*. New York: McGraw-Hill.

Marcus, S. 1974. *Engels, Manchester and the Working Class*. London: Weidenfeld and Nicholson.

Marcuse, H. 1966. "Political Preface 1966." *Eros & Civilization*. 2nd ed. London: Routledge & Kegan Paul.

Marx, K. 1906. *Capital*. Chicago: Charles Kerr & Coy.

Mitchell, B. R. 1971. *Abstract of British Historical Statistics*. London: Macmillan.

Mumford, L. 1967. *The Myth of the Machine*. London: Secker & Warburg.

Pateman, C. 1970. *Participation and Democratic Theory*. Cambridge University Press.

Rostow, W. W. 1978. *The World Economy*. London: Macmillan.

Schramm, W., ed. 1960. *The Impact of Educational T.V.* Urbana: Univ. of Illinois Press.

Schramm, W., et al. 1981. *Bold Experiment*. Palo Alto: Stanford Univ. Press.

Schumpeter, J. A. 1939. *Business Cycles*. New York: McGraw-Hill.

Singer, J. D., and Small, M. 1972. *The Wages of War 1816–1965*. New York: Wiley.

Sohn-Rethel, A. 1978. *Intellectual & Manual Labour*. London: Macmillan.

Tunzelbaum, G. N. von 1978. *Steam & British Industrialization to 1860*. Oxford: Clarendon Press.

Wertheimer, M. 1945. *Productive Thinking*. New York: Harper.

Williams, T. 1982. *Learning to Manage Our Futures*. New York: Wiley.

9
Quality of Working Life: A Paradigm in Transition

Hans van Beinum, Harvey F. Kolodny, and *Ann Armstrong*

QWL and the 80s/la QVT et les années 80, the 1981 international conference on the quality of working life, was very much a threshold event. It accommodated the past — but it also gave indications of the future. A brief introduction to that past is in order.

The development of the values and concepts of quality of working life (QWL) is based on the work of the social scientists of the Tavistock Institute of Human Relations in London, England. In the 1950s and 1960s they developed the conceptual systems that formed the foundation for our present thinking. The notion that organizations have the characteristics of open sociotechnical systems provided an intellectual framework that formed the basis for subsequent conceptual strategies. The best known of these is the sociotechnical systems approach used for analyzing work systems (Trist and Bamforth 1951; Emery 1978; Emery and Trist 1960; Trist et al. 1963).

The social scientists at the Tavistock Institute actually combined two approaches. They related open sociotechnical system thinking to the psychodynamic understanding of group processes, but they also developed a distinct professional position vis-à-vis the client system, a position that is based on the recognition that the relationship with the client system should be one of joint involvement and shared responsibility. In this way, the object is recognized as being foremost a subject. The concept and practice of "working through" illustrate this orientation (Bion 1959).

The Tavistock initiatives stimulated activities in other parts of the world. U.S. researchers began to challenge the effectiveness of jobs designed to scientific management principles (Davis 1957; Turner and Lawrence 1965). Some exciting initiatives in the United States focused on the total design of new plants, such as the well-known General Foods dog food plant in Topeka, Kansas (Walton 1972).

In Norway and Sweden in the 1960s and the early 1970s developments toward industrial democracy were of pathfinding significance. The approach taken in Scandinavia, termed "direct industrial democracy,"[1] was one of action research and action learning and, as such, was a continuation of the Tavistock approach. By the mid-1970s, it became increasingly clear that the meaning of quality of working life might be more than it appeared on the surface; that it might, in fact, be a new organizational paradigm (Emery 1978).

Sociotechnical systems analysis developed further and strongly as an effective tool for analysis and (re)design. However, a note of caution seems appropriate: some developments in sociotechnical thinking and practice seem disconnected from the very criteria used to judge the sociotechnical attributes of the work system. In other words, these developments appear not to be predicated on the understanding of the work system as being essentially an open system. They have become another sophisticated engineering methodology in which choice in (re)design is circumscribed and dictated by external experts. Should this kind of sociotechnical systems approach continue to evolve in its disassociative way, unconnected to the values underlying the process of human choice, there is a real possibility that it will collude with the old work paradigm and, as a result, become not much more than a sophisticated tool for improving the existing paradigm based on closed system thinking.

Paralleling the sociotechnical systems thinking in the 1970s was the development of the meaning of the causal texture of the environment, that is, a conceptual map distinguishing between different levels of complexity of the environment, the turbulent environment being the emerging one (Emery and Trist 1965). This breakthrough in open systems thinking was of paramount importance for the further conceptual development of QWL as well as for its practical application. It provided an insight that was essential for understanding the process of active organizational adaptation (Emery 1977).

A very important evolutionary step took place in Australia where Fred and Merrelyn Emery developed the participative (re)design approach (Emery and Emery 1976). This method reintroduces the central position of the process of "working through" in organizational choice. Furthermore, the Emerys, with their development of the search conference (Emery and Emery 1976; M. Emery 1982), provided another missing link. Participative (re)design and search are interdependent and complementary methods based on the values of QWL. By mobilizing the knowledge and commitment of the members of an organization, active participative planning becomes an ongoing learning process and the basic strategy for relating to turbulent environments in a proactive and adaptive manner. By recognizing, mobilizing, and developing the expertise from within the system, it becomes possible to integrate the sociotechnical and the open system characteristics on the conceptual, professional, and operational levels.

By the early 1980s a wide range of activities associated with the new paradigm of work was taking place not only in Western Europe and North America, but throughout the world. The timing was opportune for the first open international conference on the quality of working life.

THE MEANINGS OF THE TORONTO CONFERENCE

QWL and the 80s was a highly successful conference. The advertising material stated that it was "for managers, workers, trade unionists, professionals and others interested in and committed to improving the quality of working life. . . ." It also invited those who were new to the quality of working life field. They all came: the managers, the academics, the trade unionists, the consultants, the students, the representatives of QWL agencies and centers and productivity institutes. There were about 1,700 people in all.

Why did so many attend? Were there some common elements that attracted them, even though they came representing different constituencies with very different long-term goals? Can we attach some set of meanings to the conference that might explain this sudden explosion of popularity for a concept that has only slowly been achieving recognition and acceptance, particularly in North America?

The meaning of an event depends on the context being used; therefore, when we discuss the various meanings of the Toronto conference, we have to make clear which context we have in mind. We can look at the conference from at least three different perspectives:

- the meaning of the conference as a total phenomenon, as an historical event;
- the meaning of the conference for different categories of participants (e.g., unions, management, academics), each of which perceives the conference in the context of its own role;
- the meaning of the conference on an individual level, as a very personal experience. On this level the meaning is determined by specific personal and local factors. As the explanation of this dimension would take us well beyond the scope of this chapter we will not pursue it further here.

If we look at the conference as a total event, we can see that it affirmed the fundamental values underlying quality of working life and at the same time reflected the way QWL notions and values are being dealt with by various groups in society. In other words, the conference provided the societal and historical context of the development of quality of working life. We can distinguish various levels of appreciation:

- The conference was foremost a "flocking" conference, analogous to the flocking of bird populations that assemble from time to time in order to get a sense of the environment and the balance between their population and the resources for survival. The timing, the place, and the design of the Toronto conference was right. The field had developed such that it was necessary for the "QWL population" to come together to sense the field; to learn about new theoretical, methodological, and especially practical developments; to examine problems; and to assess the challenges and above all to get a sense of direction.

- The conference was also a significant "political" event. For the first time societal stakeholders, that is, management, labor, and government, met in an international setting. The public statements by the Canadian and the Ontario governments were more substantive than the usual conference ritual. They reflected, in this particular case, real and very visible commitment.

- The conference provided assurance and reassurance by creating a supportive, stimulating, and nourishing environment. It contributed to the legitimization of quality of working life. It brought it into the open as a major public concern.

- The conference showed an important shift away from the almost exclusive academic concern with the meaning of quality of working life to a development where quality of working life is dealt with in the real world of daily practice. This shift, and the way it manifested itself at the conference, is of great significance as it shows the new concerns, new questions and, above all, the gaps and voids in the field. Consequently, it gave indications of future developments.

- There was another shift, this one away from primarily being concerned with initiating quality of working life projects, programs, experiments, and pilot studies to a much wider set of activities designed to sustain and diffuse them. The questions were no longer whether or not to engage in quality of working life, but rather "how to" develop quality of working life.

At the conference, democratic values were heralded as the primary premise of quality of working life. These values have of course significant implications for all concerned. For while the values were for the most part not specifically stated, different formulations that underlay them were repeatedly advanced. For instance, we learned that we needed, again, "to learn to learn"; and that we had to do so by having more confidence in our own perceptions (Emery 1981). Such a process is a necessary antecedent for effective self-management. Knowledge is thus seen to reside, not in the other, but in the self.

Such an epistemological shift, a shift in the way knowledge is developed, is radical. It is a theoretical argument that challenges the scientific logic of the empiricist, the experimenter, the gatherer of facts and data. In the words of Fred Emery, "whilst the space-time of activity may be Euclidean (viz., linear), the space-time of perception, and hence cognition, is non-Euclidean" (1981, p. 27).[2] We are thus able to learn from our own perceptions and experience. Our sense data allow us to survive, to order the "buzzing blooming confusion" of the universe. We are all thus somewhat expert as knowledge emerges only as we perceive the universe. Social knowledge then emerges as we develop and share our collective perceptions.

Such an epistemology can and does destroy the classical educational paradigm. In that sense, it is an epistemology of freedom. Our education has served, ironically, to block our self-management by creating the specialist, the expert. "[Our] educational institutions [now] . . . have taken over the role of the church in Aquinas' century . . . " (Emery 1981, p. 30).

In an attempt to counter the potent antidemocratic course of our education, participative processes such as the search conference have been developed so that we might learn, together, to trust our perceptions of the universe. Once we reclaim our own expertise and truly govern ourselves, we can expect an astonishing revolution of knowledge.

MANAGEMENT, LABOR, AND OTHERS

We may also consider the meaning of the conference from the viewpoints of the different groups that participated. Despite some quite different end goals, the different constituencies found themselves for the most part able to participate in common because they shared a common set of values and beliefs, and they took common approaches to the accomplishment of their long-term goals. However, they were also at the conference to pursue their particular ends.

In a Western world badly buffeted by declining productivity and an inability to compete, and beset by charges of poor quality products and workmanship, many managers see the quality of working life area as a possible panacea, a path toward better solutions to organizational problems. The operating environments of many organizations are marked by increasing turbulence, by states of "contextual commotion." There are many interdependencies, much complexity, and much uncertainty. The technocratic bureaucracy is not designed to adapt to these conditions but to those of a more stable context. As a matter of economic and indeed societal survival, our organizations must discover the principles and parameters of a new organizational paradigm. It will have to be organic, adaptive, and innovative if it is to survive.

The creation of such a paradigm of work represents "a discontinuity" by which society leaps into a new moral order of collaboration, of quality of working life. Quality of working life approaches seek to empower workers by making them more resourceful and innovative. Their organizations become, in turn, better equipped to survive in time of turbulence because they are capable of engaging in productive, transactional exchanges with their environment.

Warily, worriedly, both management and labor have approached the QWL process — too timid, sometimes, to try, too much wounded by malevolent environments to walk away from the process. Some have committed themselves completely, engaged themselves fully — some companies and some unions. Others wait, attend conferences, listen to success stories, and begin to believe that there may be some answers for them here, some solutions to their problems, some stimuli to create new ideas, some development of innovative organizational arrangements capable of responding to the buffeting of increasingly turbulent environments.

The dangers associated with the search for a quick fix are all too apparent. For employee involvement to work, management must examine its sacred cows. It must be prepared to forfeit its residual rights — many of its "managerial prerogatives" — and to do so by specifying precisely its rights and obligations. If management desires joint consultation in areas where it has concerns, it must also engage in joint consultation prior to, for example, the proposed introduction of new technology.

The accelerating development of information technology has done much recently to transform and shape the operating environment. Automation is now economically and technically feasible for many organizations. As its unit cost decreases it will be even more widely used in the work place. The resulting human implications are significant, particularly for those currently performing clerical or professional work. Automation has the potential to "re-skill" or "de-skill" workers; it may liberate or alienate workers; and it may increase or decrease flexibility in the work place. Automation thus creates both awesome opportunities and alarming threats.

Information technology, while it is all-pervasive, is especially amenable to being shaped by "social criteria" (Walton 1981). As its unit cost continues to decline, we should be able to develop and implement efficient and effective "software intensive" solutions. Workers can be cautiously optimistic about such technology as its adverse effects can be countered by our social value structure and, for the unionized, by the collective bargaining process. Some presenters, however, argued that such a stance is dangerously naive. Some organizations in North America such as American Telephone and Telegraph have recently taken the lead by instituting a process whereby union and management together review new technology prior to its introduction. Many organizations in Scandinavia have been doing this for some time. More generally, some sort of system "to grow" our own technology is required so that both the social and the technical systems can evolve dynamically. Better evaluation methodologies are needed to assess the social, technical, and financial dimensions of information technology.

Many unions remain very wary of automation even when it is introduced under the aegis of QWL. QWL initiatives too are often suspect, perceived to be manipulative and destructive of trade unionism. If such initiatives are to succeed, both union and management must squarely confront and meet several substantial challenges (Cohen-Rosenthal 1981). Unionists must be prepared to reappraise their traditional stance on the seniority and classification provisions now in many collective agreements. Such a stance has served, albeit unwittingly, to reinforce the bureaucratic rigidity of the work place.

Some trade unionists are enthusiastic advocates of QWL. Inasmuch as QWL entails the right of workers to participate significantly in decision making, "it requires sincere, steadfast commitment" from management and labor alike. QWL can and has enhanced the dignity of the worker and is, as such, consistent with and represents an extension of the historic mission of trade unionism. The negotiated labor contract provisions, however, are to remain inviolate so that QWL processes do not abrogate the gains made through collective bargaining. Other presenters pointed out that labor and management are not distinct but interdependent interests.[3] They must be able to reach compromise, and they must come together on a common ground to do so. Thus, their relationship is not so much an adversarial one as one of mutual dependence. QWL processes in such a context can serve to increase the power of all the participants. "The Maginot Line view of industrial relations . . . is an imaginary view of the nature and possibilities of power and authority in the workplace." More specifically, participation in QWL processes may gain the union access to information, higher visibility, better grievance handling procedures, increased worker satisfaction, and improved health and safety. The union, however, may risk coop tation, contract violations, and intraunion conflicts. "[Real] situations [will necessarily differ, involving] varying degrees of the benefits and headaches."

Management comes to QWL with some traditions of experimentation with new approaches. That is, after all, a central management task. It will not be easy because a new paradigm of work means much more than implementing a new set of methods. Still, there is some background of changing, some experience with challenging the status quo, even among the very cautious and conservative.

For unions the commitment is greater. So much is at stake. Their experience informs them to go slow, to be wary, to be careful who you trust. Given that tradition, some would rather not confront decisions about the work itself immediately, but would rather work first with other issues where the need is at least as great and perhaps more immediate. Occupational health and safety concerns are one such set of issues.

Occupational health and safety concerns were broadly explored at the conference and seemed to be of particular interest to unionists and policy makers. The work place has "multiple stressors" and thus requires a holistic process of reform. Only then can a work environment of "zero risk" be created. Some presenters felt that conventional legislative approaches to occupational health and safety have had minimal effect. Such approaches are both limited and limiting because they concentrate only on those concerns that can be readily legislated. The process was described as a "passive" one in which only the few publicly funded experts are involved.

It was felt that an alternative and strategic approach to occupational health and safety must be developed, and that it must be predicated on participation by the workers since it is they who are the most knowledgeable about their particular health and safety needs. Such legislation should be two pronged: it should require conformance to and improvement of standards. A planning, action, and evaluation program must be created by each organization to improve the conditions in its work place.

Union leaders and union members came to the Toronto conference in numbers greater than had attended such a conference before. It would be misleading, however, to read into their numbers any collective statement about commitment. They were, for the most part, ambivalent, particularly with regard to the motivation of management. They were interested because QWL values and ideals were of the kind they themselves had always espoused. The leaders came because many of their members were either curious about or committed to QWL initiatives. They also wanted to explore the relationship between QWL and health and safety initiatives. Furthermore, microelectronics had reared its ominous head, and the potential impact on white collar jobs was frightening. They were both threatened and excited because QWL approaches could, in time, affect the democratic processes within the ranks of their own unions. And they were suspicious because so many managers were in attendance and some came from organizations that had clear histories of being unfriendly to the union movement.

Management and labor were the primary constituencies at the conference, but they were not the only ones. The public sector comprises an increasingly large set of people with an abiding interest in the quality of working life. It was strongly represented at the conference by employers, employees, and unions. The public sector shares many of the long-term goals of the private sector and many of the same concerns about employee involvement. Of particular interest to public sector participants is the possibility that quality of working life approaches may improve the design of many clerical tasks and provide a way to work around the pitfalls clearly evident in so many current conversions to the "office of the future." They view quality of working life as a potential means to avoid the kind of work arrangements that resulted in so much alienation and job dissatisfaction in the private sector where designs were impelled by technological and mechanistic considerations alone.

For outside consultants at the conference, quality of working life is a vehicle that allows them to engage in a challenging new arena. It is an opportunity to redesign work and the role relationships of people in a manner consistent with the humanistic values to which most of them ascribe. However, the meaning of the term "expert" is changing in the quality of working life field, and outside consultants will be no more immune to those changes than will inside specialists and experts.

For academics, quality of working life provides an opportunity to understand a new paradigm of work, a system that elaborates how people, jobs, and organizations can and should be put together. Academics are beginning to realize that the concepts underlying QWL provide a new way of thinking that addresses the deficiencies of bureaucratic form in general, and scientific management in particular.

The QWL agencies and associations share many of the aspirations of the academics. However, they have yet another interest. They are particularly concerned with the subject of diffusion: how quality of working life activities are sustained; how QWL information and experiences are disseminated; and how QWL interventions spread beyond the innovators to include still larger segments of society.

There were many students at the conference. While their long-term goals were difficult to discern, it appeared that most were excited by the concept of a new paradigm of work.

COMMON PROCESSES

The long-term goals of these different constituencies are not clear at present. In the long run, it could well be that they will have increasing difficulty coming together to carry out shared activities. Some have suggested that the QWL and the 80s Conference may have been the last large, open QWL conference. Their prediction is that those interested in QWL will have to divide up into groups that have more commonality around long-term goals. If this view reflects reality, which we are not inclined to believe, then it would be indicative of maladaptive behavior, for example, segmentation, dissociation, and superficiality on a societal level. Ironically, such maladaptive behavior among constituencies would be the result of the pursuit of the active adaptive strategy of QWL by each of them independently.

For many, however, the common values that brought 1700 people to Toronto prevail. They continue to offer some basis for coming together in common cause. So, too, do the design and implementation processes used in common by the different constituencies interested in QWL. It is the immediacy of the different constituencies' interests in QWL processes and their shared values that encourage them to meet in common, as they did so successfully at this conference.

The processes of design and implementation enable and require us to develop a statement of organizational principle to motivate and guide our efforts. They then enable us to create the requisite transitional organizational forms through and by which we must further design. The basic building block of these processes becomes "the self-managing unit." It must evolve from a process of joint design. Joint design or joint optimization ensure that the technical system will complement the social system. Teams charged with the responsibility of joint design must be granted the authority for decision making, and this process must be carried on participatively. "Process [thus] is the key": it is the necessary, if not sufficient, antecedent for effective organizational adaption to the moving ground, the turbulent field.

The attendance patterns at the conference reflected this. The "how to" sessions were all full. The sessions dealing with the changing roles of supervisors were equally crowded. While union attendance was not greater than 250 people, most of the union-oriented sessions attracted between 400 and 500 people each despite the fact that there were as many as 15 other sessions offered at the same time. Some of the union concerns revolved around the effects on future employment of increasing automation in the work place.

THE DEVELOPMENT OF QWL UNDERSTANDING

It is rather clear that the main thread running through our discussion in this chapter is formed by the fact that the field has shifted. To summarize:

- QWL is not an academic subject any longer but is becoming a matter of every day organizational concern.
- The focus of QWL is widening and includes the processes of sustaining and diffusing QWL.
- The discussion is no longer on whether or not QWL, but on "how" to develop QWL.

All this suggests that we are facing a methodological question. We believe that the real meaning of the conference therefore has to be understood in that particular context.

The significance of the conference can be seen not only in what the conference was but also in what it was not. The conference showed a gap, a void. Something was missing. There was an inability to deal, at least in the formal program, with the "how to" question in a new way. It became clear that traditional sociotechnical systems thinking can only deal in a limited way with the basic questions of ongoing processes of organizational change. Little space was given to some of the psychodynamics one encounters in sustaining and diffusing quality of working life.

Phenomena such as the use of the organizational characteristics as a defense mechanism against anxiety, or the necessity for a transitional object for learning in organizations, or union-management collaboration as a defense against QWL, did not receive any attention.

Another obvious void had to do with the absence of dealing with the political meaning of quality of working life. The conference could not yet cope with the fact that all important societal issues such as quality of working life are also political issues.

Are we waiting for the social sciences to provide us with new theoretical insights and novel scientific methods? Are we waiting for a new generation of experts? One can argue that academics, researchers, and theoreticians rarely lead the field in the social sciences. Notable exceptions are the work of such people as Fred Emery and Phil Herbst, but in general academics tend to follow the initiatives of leading edge developments in organizational and social change in specific settings and then cast these innovations into conceptual frameworks, models, and theories that are intended to be generalizable beyond the particular case under study.

If we look back to the origins of quality of working life as described briefly at the start of this chapter we can to some extent observe this phenomenon. Early experiences with therapeutic groups in the United Kingdom (Bion) and group dynamics in the United States (Lewin) were coupled to the Tavistock studies carried out in British coal fields to generate the first sociotechnical systems concepts. Further experimentation in India, Australia, and Scandinavia allowed continued development of the theoretical base.

Suddenly, in the 1970s and 1980s, the interest in quality of working life type activity became widespread. But in general the theoretical base lags behind this surge of interest because, with the exception of Scandinavia, the amount of recent direct industrial democracy experience is still relatively limited. The Scandinavians are just beginning to document their experiences,[4] but North American experiences lag behind these considerably. As such, theoretical development that might be drawn from North American experience will not advance until better field experience is obtained.

If this assumption is correct, then using Figure 9.1 we can follow and project a cycle of development. Stimulated by existing theories, by some leading edge developments, as well as by some academics and consultants, many North American managers became interested in and engaged in new initiatives in the area of work design. Those initiatives, in turn, attracted the interest of unions and their members. To some extent this explains the high level of concentration at the Toronto conference on "how to" sessions, union issues, and supervisory discussions. Continuing on with the diagram, as this interest is translated into action, the specialists will become even more involved, developing training packages, compensation systems and other new support systems, and attempting to diffuse the learning and ex-

FIGURE 9.1.

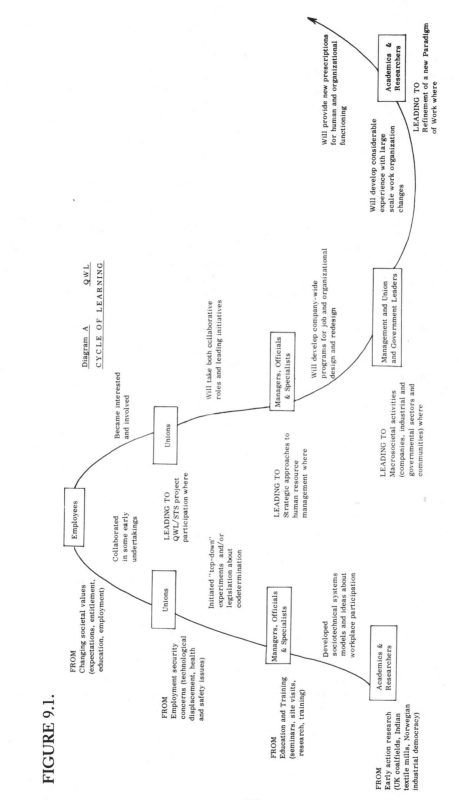

Diagram A   QWL
CYCLE OF LEARNING

FROM
Changing societal values
(expectations, entitlement,
education, employment)

FROM
Employment security
concerns (technological
displacement, health
and safety issues)

FROM
Education and Training
(seminars, site visits,
research, training)

FROM
Early action research
(UK coalfields, Indian
textile mills, Norwegian
industrial democracy)

Employees

Unions

Collaborated
in some early
undertakings

LEADING TO
QWL/STS project
participation where

Initiated "top-down"
experiments and/or
legislation about
codetermination

Managers, Officials
& Specialists

Developed
sociotechnical systems
models and ideas about
workplace participation

Academics &
Researchers

Became interested
and involved

Unions

Will take both collaborative
roles and leading initiatives

Managers, Officials
& Specialists

LEADING TO
Strategic approaches to
human resource
management where

Will develop company-wide
programs for job and organizational
design and redesign

Management and Union
and Government Leaders

LEADING TO
Macrosocietal activities
(companies, industrial and
governmental sectors and
communities) where

Will develop considerable
experience with large
scale work organization
changes

Will provide new prescriptions
for human and organizational
functioning

Academics &
Researchers

LEADING TO
Refinement of a new Paradigm
of Work where

150

perience to other parts of their organizations. Managers, too, will shift their involvement. From a concentration on "getting started," it will move to a broader view that will include quality of working life in human resources management and other strategic level issues.

Only as a significant number of initiatives begin to work down the right side of the diagram will enough experience be generated to allow further significant conceptual advancement, probably in areas dealing with theories of change, autonomous group functioning, diffusion, and the entire subject of participation.

Only then will the initiatives broaden out to include macrosocial levels as well. Eric Trist (1981) has referred to this kind of a cycle as development at the level of the primary work system; in whole organization systems; and at the macrosocial level.

If we accept Figure 9.1 as a reasonable model of how learning in this field has taken place and will continue to take place, then a new cycle will begin based on an expanded new base of good field experience and data about processes and outcomes. From this, academics, researchers, and other "experts" will develop new concepts and theories to fill out and develop further a comprehensive new paradigm of work.

Figure 9.1 is, however, a conventional view of knowledge development, and in this view the traditional "expert" role is highly significant. Fred Emery (1981) suggests that this creates a dilemma for us because it keeps us dependent on experts. His experience with work democratization leads him to conclude that workers and managers come to distrust that expertise at the same time they are dependent on it. As such, how we learn becomes a crucial ingredient in how we change organizations. Emery argues that the dilemma cannot be resolved unless "we go beyond the challenge of the organizational paradigm to challenge the educational paradigm" (1981, p. 25).

Emery argues further that we are confronted with a new educational paradigm that recognizes that human beings are marvelously well adapted to learn from their individual experience of the real non-Euclidean world. It changes radically our notion of the role of experts.

> Within the new paradigm everyone is expert to some degree from the moment their experiences allow them some direct perception of the invariants in the environment with which they were interacting. [Emery 1981, p. 28]

> When the common people 'invent' theories about their world in their naively realistic way they are engaged in the same kind of theory making as the scientists. [Emery 1981, p. 30]

These "real" experts, the workers, were not at the Toronto conference. The people who in actual fact experience and manage on an existential level the process of change in the work place were not there to participate. If theirs is the kind of knowledge development necessary to cope with the next phase in the development of QWL, then it clearly could not have taken place at this particular conference.

The development of appropriate social science knowledge, then, may not be the result of the linear process suggested in Figure 9.1. It is more likely to emerge as a result of a nonlinear process characterized by a high level of interaction and joint involvement of workers, managers, unionists, academics, and researchers—a blending of Euclidean and non-Euclidean thinking.

We believe that these gaps in the Toronto conference were unavoidable. We believe that it was historically not possible to avoid a design and a structure that reflected a social system that was still linked to the old paradigm as shown in the thematic approach taken in the design of the conference. On the other hand, the conference quite purposefully created all kinds of open spaces, different kinds of "empty areas" in which the new paradigm could emerge and where more appropriate temporary social systems and new ways of learning could be accommodated.

We stated earlier that the real meaning of the conference was not only reflected in what it was not, but also in what it was. The latter refers to the fact that there was a conference within a conference. By this we mean that the great number of simultaneous sessions of different kinds combined with the formal open program created a space that was both psychological and social. Furthermore, it was a safe space in which people could interact, participate, and explore without having to be an expert in the traditional sense. The conference in this space was the conference of the "barefoot social scientist."[5]

The Toronto conference was clearly a threshold event. Whether it was an indication of future progress, a repunctuation in a process of positive developments, can probably be seen in the design of future conferences. Will they accommodate a new educational paradigm as well as a new organizational one? Will they focus primarily on the kind of participants who are personally involved in their own QWL? It is likely that future conferences will accommodate these perspectives not so much by bringing workers to the conference, but by bringing the conference to the work place.

This statement is not only intended as a metaphor but also very much as a real possibility. It is based on the belief that if one wishes to increase one's understanding of QWL processes, one has to do so through work and by learning to trust one's perceptions of working experiences. We need new forms of interaction and participative real life learning in which people can meet and learn while working—where learning is done with and within the field.

The Toronto conference has shown that the time is ripe to take this next step.

NOTES

1. "Direct industrial democracy" refers to employee participation in their own work places. In this type of democracy people can have direct and personal influence on their work environment. "Representative or indirect democracy" deals with the kind of employee participation whereby people can exercise influence through others, such as their elected representatives—as is the case with many codetermination systems.

2. Emery's use of the terms "Euclidean" and "non-Euclidean" are explained in his article in this book (Emery 1981). Simply stated, the former refers to predictable, linear causal relationships, e.g., if A occurs then B follows. Non-Euclidean assumes a nonlinear situation where, as in the case of cognition, for example, understanding might come from a variety of inputs whose interactions to produce new understanding are likely not predictable.

3. This point and subsequent quotations in this paragraph are from a special session at the QWL and the 80s Conference entitled "Health and Safety and Workers' Participation," with Bjorn Gustavsen (Work Research Institute, Oslo, Norway) and Robert Sass (Saskatchewan Labour Department, Canada).

4. See a variety of publications in English by the Swedish Employers Confederation (SAF) with different authors (e.g., Agurén, Edgren, Lindestad, Lindholm, Norstedt). Recently Swedish trade unions, the Swedish Trade Union Confederation (LO) in particular, and The Swedish Working Life Center have begun to publish considerable material in English in this area. See also Gyllenhammer (1977), Emery and Thorsrud (1976), and a range of publications in English by Scandinavian academics and researchers (e.g., Björk, Elden, Engelstad, Gardell, Gulowson, Gustavsen, Hansson, Herbst, Karlsson, Qvale, Sandberg, Stymne, Thorsrud).

5. The term comes from Merrelyn Emery's paper entitled, "The Theory of Diffusion," August 1981, given at the conference. The term "barefoot social scientist" attempts to describe a "new and proper role" for social scientists that can be filled by people actively involved in learning their own activities and not only by those who have been trained in traditional positivistic science.

REFERENCES

Bion, W. R. 1959. *Experiences in Groups*. London: Tavistock Publications.

Cohen-Rosenthal, Edward. 1980. "Should Unions Participate in Quality of Working Life Activities." In *Quality of Working Life: The Canadian Scene* 3, no. 1.

Davis, L. E. 1957. "Toward a Theory of Job Design." *Journal of Industrial Engineering* 8: 305-9.

Emery, F. E. 1977. *Futures We Are In*. Leiden: Martinus Nijhoff.

Emery F. E. 1978. *The Emergence of a New Paradigm of Work*. Centre for Continuing Education, Australian National University, chap. 4, "Characteristics of Socio-Technical Systems" (1959), pp. 38–86.

Emery, F. E. 1981. "Sociotechnical Foundations for a New Social Order." In this volume.

Emery, F. E., and Emery, M. 1976. "Participative Design: Work and Community Life." In *Democracy at Work*, Fred Emery and Einar Thorsrud, eds. Leiden: Martinus Nijhoff, Formal Sciences Division.

Emery, F. E., and Thorsrud, E. 1976. *Democracy at Work*. Leiden: Martinus Nijhoff.

Emery, F. E. and Trist, E. 1960. "Socio-Technical Systems." In *Management Science, Models and Techniques*, C. W. Churchman and M. Verhurst, eds. London: Pergamon.

Emery, F. E., and Trist, E. 1965. "The Causal Texture of Organizational Environments." *Human Relations* 18:21–32.

Emery, Merrelyn. 1982. *Searching—For New Directions—In New Ways—For New Times*. Revised 1982, forthcoming. (First Edition, 1976)

Gyllenhammar, Pehr. 1977. *People at Work*. Mass.: Addison-Wesley.

Trist, E. L. 1981. "The Evolution of Socio-Technical Systems." Occasional paper, The Ontario QWL Centre, no. 2, June, Toronto.

Trist, E. L., and Bamforth, K. W. 1951. "Some Social and Psychological Consequences of the Longwall Method of Coal-Getting." *Human Relations* 4: 3–38.

Trist, E. L.; Higgins, G. W.; Murray, H.; and Pollock, A. B. 1963. *Organisational Choice: Capabilities of Groups at the Coal Face Under Changing Technologies*. London: Tavistock Publications.

Turner, A. N., and Lawrence, Paul R. 1965. *Industrial Jobs and the Worker*. Boston: Harvard University, Division of Research, Graduate School of Business Administration.

Walton, Richard E. 1972. "How to Counter Alienation in the Plant." *Harvard Business Review* (Nov/Dec.): 70–81.

Walton, Richard E. 1981. "Social Choice in the Development of Advanced Information Technologies." In this volume.

10
Six Early Cases

Ann Armstrong

As the introduction to this book suggests, the conference QWL and the 80's/la QVT et les années 80 brought a new perspective to the forefront in the development of the quality of working life field as the interests of practitioners became paramount. The Toronto conference emphasized "how to" over and over again. Managers asked how to get started. Union leaders did not dwell excessively on whether or not to take part in QWL processes, but rather were more vocal about what to be concerned with *while* taking part.

This chapter is based on a sample of some of the "how to" stories presented at the conference. Excerpts from six cases were selected for their diversity and for the lessons to be learned from them. In the former category I tried to include a broad spectrum of contexts, experiences, and understandings of QWL, some very positive, others somewhat uncertain. In the category of learning I searched for common precepts, or working rules, that cut across the six cases to provide a preliminary synthesis of the concerns associated with starting a QWL process.

The reader will detect common concepts in the case presentations. But she or he will also notice a very pragmatic orientation in the actions of the actors described. As such, the six case excerpts represent a kind of praxis whereby theory and practice are synthesized.

ADMINISTRATIVE AND CLERICAL OFFICERS ASSOCIATION*

The Administrative and Clerical Officers Association (ACOA) has a membership of approximately 50,000 people in the management grades of the

---

*Davies, 1981.

federal public service of Australia. Established at the turn of the century, it had been regarded for years as a staff association rather than a trade union, and had enjoyed a comfortable relationship with its employer. During the 1970s, both the environment and the membership of ACOA began to change rapidly. The structure of ACOA was seen to have become inappropriate for an environment of increasing turbulence in which political and legislative measures were introduced to diminish the public service, and thereby the job security of the public servants, and to restrict union activity. In June 1980 the federal executive of ACOA created a task force to engage ACOA in a process of participative planning. The task force comprised "a deep slice" of six members and officials and one external consultant.

The task force was charged with the responsibility of comparing ACOA's organizational objectives with those of other unions, and of investigating and making recommendations on, among others, the structure and effectiveness of decision making, the communication between the organizational subunits, and the administrative and planning capabilities of ACOA. A comprehensive review process in which the rank and file could participate was seen to be vital. The task force received a commitment of $40,000 (Australian) and was required to make its final report to the executive meeting scheduled for June 1981 so that an agenda could be prepared for the federal conference in November 1981.

The task force first met in September 1980 and participated in a search process. As a result, a five-phase plan emerged, predicated on several critical assumptions. They were that the expertise and experience necessary to transform ACOA lay within its rank and file and its officials and that the best way to ascertain the views of ACOA's members was "to consult with them." As well, it was desired that those who were to make decisions about ACOA should be among those directly involved in the generation of alternatives; that there be at least one learning cycle in the task force's work; that the role of the task force be a facilitative and coordinating one; that the process be as open as possible and that it allow ACOA in the future to use both participative and representative practices and structures. The five-phase plan entailed (1) consultation with the national executive, the branches, and the membership by such practices as search conferences, discussion groups involving members drawn by lot, and the solicitation of contributions from members; (2) preparation of a discussion paper; (3) further consultation; (4) a report to the executive meeting scheduled for June 1981; and (5) the federal conference scheduled for November 1981 to determine what changes, if any, should be made to the organization of ACOA. It was anticipated that the many recommendations on substantive constitutional reform for ACOA, generated by the five-phase plan, would be passed at the federal conference.

SUDAN RAILWAYS CORPORATION*

An executive of the World Bank insisted that a sociotechnical study be performed for a proposed locomotive maintenance workshop at Sennar in the Sudan. The completion of such a study was specified as the antecedent condition for the bank's loan of construction funds to the Democratic Republic of Sudan, a developing country suffering from acute shortages of fuel, food, and housing, and with an 80 percent illiteracy rate. The Sudan Railways Corporation (SRC) therefore engaged several consultants to perform a sociotechnical study with the express object of designing "a work organization that would provide improved productivity and quality of work" (Ketchum 1981). The design was to allow an initial service capacity for 80 locomotives with a capability of expansion to 150.

The sociotechnical study first involved a comparative analysis between the operating environment of a U.S. workshop and that of an existing SRC facility at Atbara. The environment of the proposed workshop site at Sennar was also assessed. At Atbara, a task force and steering committee for the study were created. The study diagnosed many complex problems affecting the performance of the Atbara workshop. They were the unavailability of needed spare parts; the brain and skill drain without adequate replacement; excessively bureaucratic ideologies, structures, and rituals; demoralized managers and workers, and the general lack of autonomy in decision making at SRC. These conclusions formed the basis of the recommended design.

The recommended design for the Sennar workshop was predicated on a statement of organizational principle that affirms "that it is everybody's job to ... teach ... to learn and ... to maintain an atmosphere where learning takes place" (Ketchum 1981). The design therefore included a "planned (or purposive) redundancy" whereby workers would spend two days a week in "intensive, off-the-job training" to acquire such skills as reading and writing. Other subjects included the workshop's mission and organization, safety, and elementary metallurgy. Workers and managers alike were able and expected to participate in human development.

The design was further predicated on the principle that "decisions will be made at the lowest possible level" and that "jobs will be designed to satisfy, insofar as possible, the psychological needs of individuals." Mini-shops were to be created, "discrete but fully integrated," in and by which whole tasks were to be performed. Each mini-shop was to have a precise, comprehensive articulated mission; each was to have a mechanism to gauge the realization of its mission; each was to perform a discrete, measurable trans-

---

*Ketchum, 1981.

formation; each was "(to) have exclusive turf, where possible"; each was to have a product stream and to inspect the product before passing it on; each was to be able to limit the number of workers in the mini-shop; and each was to have a relationship both with the users of its product and with the suppliers of its inputs. Mini-shops would have specialist coordinators chosen by the workers from among themselves. The pay system for the workers, now called "technicians," was designed to reward "in-depth development." As well, the need for a flexible, plant-wide support team was recognized.

SHELL INTERNATIONAL PETROLEUM COMPANY LIMITED*

Several critical problems were found to plague a few of the functional divisions in the head office of the Shell International Petroleum Company Limited (Shell). Productivity had dropped in the production of reports, one of the divisions' principal activities. Various automated systems were not integrated and, as a result, data processing was less than efficient. Boundaries had developed between jobs as workers suffered from the "it's not my job" syndrome. Most of the workers in the divisions, professional and secretarial alike, were insufficiently skilled in the use of the available systems. Much work continued to be performed laboriously by hand. Work was poorly planned and coordinated. Workers therefore received little, if any, job satisfaction and morale was accordingly low.

Against such a backdrop and following from a major review of the divisions, a study team was created in November 1979. It comprised four members, three drawn from the divisions and a consultant. The team was "to examine current activities within all divisions concerned with administration, data requirements and processing methods, and to consider the implications of the recent organization review in terms of future administrative requirements" (Butteriss 1981). The team was given two months in which to carry out the study and draft recommendations. The team first surveyed the administrative activities of the divisions and asked workers to highlight areas of particular concern to them and make suggestions for improvement. The use of individual and group interviews facilitated the surveying of all 200 members of the divisions.

The survey highlighted four areas of particular concern. They were: (1) the production of reports was an unduly protracted process often involving 17 stages; (2) information was independently generated without any semblance of coordination; (3) professionals were performing some secretarial

---

*Butteriss, 1981.

tasks; and (4) there was little dialogue between the divisions and the users of their services.

In an attempt to overcome these difficulties, various substantive organizational changes were recommended. Administrative work was redefined and was seen to comprise four distinct tasks: technical administrative support for the divisions; secretarial functions to support the divisions' professionals; long lead time supporting services such as the production of reports; and central services such as the telex capability.

The first two tasks were to be the responsibility of the divisions, but the latter two were to become the responsibility of a newly formed unit, Business and Information Support Services (BISS). BISS was to have three sub-units, namely, the text preparation unit, the data systems service unit, and the central services unit. As well, both operators and users of word processors were to receive special training so that they could learn to deploy the word processors more effectively. The findings of the study, completed in January 1980, were accepted by top management in March of that year. While the production of reports has become more efficient, it is not yet as efficient as it might be.

SAN FRANCISCO'S WORK IMPROVEMENT PROJECT*

The San Francisco Work Improvement Project (The Project) was motivated by the 1978 passage of Proposition 13 (a referendum to reduce state taxation) in California. Public service workers of Local 400 of the Service Employees International Union (SEIU) responded by proposing The Project as a means of improving the efficiency of service delivery throughout the city. The city's first labor-management worksite committee was created in the fall of 1978 in the medical records department of the San Francisco General Hospital. The worksite committee, initiated by the local, was an ad hoc and informal organization. Two more such committees were created, one in the radiology department of the hospital and one in the general assistance division of the Department of Social Services. The Project was able to secure funding only in early 1980. It then set out to create 12 labor-management worksite committees, steered by an advisory committee headed by a unionist and a manager as co-directors.

The first crisis arose when the worksite committee in the radiology department was dissolved. This precipitated a redesign of The Project as there were "glimpses of (its) potential" in the medical records department where "the department (was) completely turned around" (Olsen 1981). The Proj-

---

*Olsen, 1981.

ect's dilemmas at the General Hospital were then assessed. Research was initiated into the experiences of public sector labor-management committees. A consultant processing QWL experience also was engaged. As a result, a more formal multi-level structure of citywide, departmental, and worksite committees was adopted. This structure was designed to facilitate the accomplishment of The Project's principal goal of "maintaining and enhancing the quality of work life in City services during a time of severe stress."

The Project is now steered by a citywide policy committee comprised of the mayor or her designate and the heads of the participating departments and their corresponding union representatives. The committee's role is to coordinate and diffuse QWL efforts in the city. The committee, in mid-1980, drafted a "letter of commitment" in which the rights and the duties of each party were specified. The letter of commitment, as of September 1981, had not been signed. There exists so far only one departmental committee and it is in the San Francisco Housing Authority. This committee has drafted *and* signed a letter of commitment and is now engaged in the process of identifying possible areas within the authority for its first "grassroots-level" worksite committee. Other departments are now considering creating such committees. At the moment, however, only 50 or so people are involved in The Project. It has no further funding and its staff has had to resign. The future of The Project thus is most uncertain and could be "easily . . . lost in the larger turbulence of labor relations" in a city marked by "fragmentation" of administration. Nonetheless, "all the participants sincerely hope that getting The Project started will have been the hardest part" (Olsen 1981).

DEPARTMENT OF NATIONAL DEFENCE – CANADA AND THE UNION OF NATIONAL DEFENCE EMPLOYEES*

The Public Service of Canada classifies federal public servants into over 70 occupational groupings and does so on a service-wide basis encompassing people in the same class of work in *all* departments. Unions thus must represent and negotiate for people who work in many different departments while coming under the same collective agreements. Negotiations, therefore, are much removed from the realities and concerns of the many local work places. QWL initiatives in this context are seen to be one possible means of dealing with local problems at the local level.

Such initiatives are not seen in any way to be a replacement for the traditional collective bargaining process. Legislation mandating the process for federal public servants, such as the employees of the Department of Nation-

*Johnston and Porter, 1981.

al Defence (DND), limits the nature and content of bargaining. Unions cannot, for example, negotiate about the employer's hiring and firing practices, its classification of positions, any possible introduction of technological or other changes, the pension plan, or other welfare benefits. Unions cannot, in effect, negotiate about the employer's organizational control. This legislative framework precludes defense employees from entering negotiations to redress any problems in such areas and serves, therefore, as a significant catalyst for QWL initiatives. The need for quality of working life initiatives at DND has, then, been structurally stimulated.

Labor-management relations at the DND have been historically successful, marked by continued improvement and motivated by a process of consultation. DND and the Union of National Defence Employees (UNDE) have had labor-management relations committees on a few military bases since 1956. There now exist such committees both at the national and the local levels. The success of the committees prompted the union to review various approaches to democratizing the work place and, to do so, sponsored a four-day conference at which representatives from West Germany, Sweden, the Canadian Labour Congress, DND, the executive of UNDE, and an academic came together. The union concluded that it could not see itself sitting on its "Board of Directors," that is, the defense management committee or the Prime Minister's Cabinet of the federal government. However, the union did find the concept of shop floor control to be particularly appropriate. In 1978 DND was asked by the Treasury Board, the ultimate employer in the federal public service, to establish a pilot project: DND declined to participate in the experiment. Discussions continued nonetheless and, in October 1979, the national labor-management relations committee appointed a subcommittee to investigate QWL initiatives for the *civilian* workforce of DND. The subcommittee was composed of three members of UNDE and three representatives of DND.

The subcommittee first examined the applicability of a QWL program for the civilian workforce at DND. It found such a program to be both applicable and desirable. In its examinations, it also found that there were several key structural dimensions to DND that could have considerable impact on the feasibility and implementation of such a program. For example, it found that there was already an inventory of ongoing "QWL-like" activities at DND and there was a labor-management relations committee tradition.

The subcommittee concluded that it was indeed feasible to implement a QWL program. It recommended that the program be introduced into DND through the local labor-management relations committees and that it involve various educational programs. The subcommittee developed a two-fold implementation strategy: an education program for senior management and union leaders at the various commands and a similar program at local bases; and the formation of QWL subcommittees of local labor-management relations committees and the creation of a small QWL subcommittee of the national labor-management relations committee.

Recently, final departmental approval was obtained from the deputy minister and the chief of the Defence Staff. A trial was set to begin in the fall of 1981 at one base where "a collaborative and participative approach to enhancing work, the work place, and the worker" would be attempted.

COMPUTER OPERATIONS DIVISION*

The manager of the Computer Operations Division (COD) in a research development organization suggested that sociotechnical system (STS) analysis could serve as a method and a process for solving the persistent problems of operator apathy and turnover. A sociotechnical system analysis and design process can comprise five distinct steps:

- scanning the system to ascertain the mission, the boundaries, and the dilemmas of the organization;
- performing a technical analysis to identify the system throughputs;
- performing a variance control analysis;
- performing a social system analysis; and
- from the findings of such an exploratory process, designing an alternative organizational form.

STS has demonstrably improved the productivity and the quality of work life of organizations. It has been much used "in blue collar settings . . . [but] is equally effective in white collar administrative and service units" (Taylor 1981).

Previous attempts at change in the COD had been largely unsuccessful, ad hoc responses to specific complaints. Recommendations of task forces had often been ignored and COD employees had become frustrated. The COD manager recognized the value of employee participation in the analysis, design, and implementation of the STS project. She discussed the project with her subordinate managers and supervisors and then formed a steering committee. The steering committee, comprised of seven managers and supervisors, conducted a series of meetings for all COD employees to inform them of the project and the process for creating the working group. The working group, comprised of two representatives from the operator shift groups, other COD groups, and the supervisors, numbered ten with ten alternative members. The sociotechnical analysis group (STAG), in Sep-

---

*Taylor, 1981.

tember 1977, began weekly meetings to set up schedules and clarify issues. STAG recognized the need for frequent communication with fellow COD employees and therefore decided to issue weekly memos. STAG received three days of off-site training in STS analysis and team-building techniques.

STAG then performed the requisite analyses and, by the end of the sixth month, the steering committee had accepted STAG's reports on both the technical and social analyses. At about the same time, a new manager was appointed for the COD, as the original manager had been promoted. The STS analysis indicated that COD was a service organization that sought to meet a wide variety of requests from many users. Many of the requests came in at the end of the day shift and, as a result, the coordination of work over or between shifts was limited. Employees felt ill-trained and ill-regarded and were particularly irritated by compulsory weekend work. The new manager endorsed the project and supported its continuation. He saw the steering committee as useful in his period of transition and, rather than being dissolved, it was reconstituted to include him, several managers, supervisors, and STAG members. An STS design team was formed that comprised seven members from STAG and three members from management and supervision.

Five weeks after its initial meeting, the design team had drafted and distributed a proposal incorporating alternatives for the redesign of COD. Employees of COD then discussed and responded to the proposal. The design team collected the responses and developed an interim proposal for circulation and consideration. The COD manager and the steering committee continued to review and comment on the interim proposal. The design team wrote a second draft to which the manager made significant changes. Ultimately, he did accept in principle the original design and took responsibility for its implementation. The final design involved a reorganization of COD and some relocation of hardware and personnel. The implementation process took over one year and involved all the members of COD. The manager invited all COD employees to bid for the newly created role of shift supervisor. He then selected two senior supervisors whose task it became to plan and implement the remainder of the design. Employee training was a key, if belated, dimension of the implementation process.

Three years after the implementation, management reports continuing favorable results — the final product has increased in quality; planning and operations management have improved; turnover has decreased from 40 percent per annum (or 3.3 percent per month) to 1 percent per month; and morale appears to have improved. COD has had an opportunity to evaluate the design and modify it. It chose to maintain the design and thereby endorsed and demonstrated its worth.

LEARNINGS FROM THESE CASES

We learn from these cases that our efforts to transform the work place are always tiring and stressful. Our efforts resemble infantry work by which we can proceed only haltingly.[1] Our efforts are further thwarted as we have so much to learn and to unlearn. We enter a Pandora's box out of which there exists no clear or simple passage. Change does not occur readily in any organization: even in democratic organizations efforts at change may be fiercely resisted and the status quo defended. (The ACOA case, in particular, alerts us to the necessity of trade unions becoming more participative in their own processes and structures if they are to demand and realize a truly democratic work place). Change, by its very nature, is uncertain and, for most of us, frightening. If our attempts at change are to succeed, the context, both within and without, must be appropriately stimulating and supporting. Environmental turbulence acts as a propelling force and can do much to mold the goals, the structures, and the processes of an organization. Our existential assumptions and societal values can likewise propel us.

QWL efforts often take considerably longer than expected. We often thus become both frustrated and disappointed as we are wont "[to expect] Disneyland in three weeks."[2] QWL efforts demand the intensive and extensive commitment of all our resources. We must work patiently and resolutely for our QWL: QWL does not allow us "to quit working-and-live."

The process of design, or redesign, is often a tortuous one, rarely following the sequences indicated by the models of scholars. We seldom, in practice, pass through the prescribed phases of involvement, agreement, negotiation, planning, building, and evaluating when we attempt to restructure work.[3] We often engage only in some of the processes and do so simultaneously rather than sequentially.

Process, nonetheless, remains critical for the successful initiation, maintenance, and persistence of diffusion of our QWL efforts. All six cases illustrate some common processes for the initiation of change. (They inform us not at all on how we can best sustain or diffuse our efforts. The change efforts have, so far, no real past and are, as such, embryonic, novel, and possessing an uncertain future.) All created some sort of temporary group, be it a task force or a committee, at the outset of their change efforts. These groups performed considerable anticipatory planning and did so principally by drawing on the organization's internal resources. Some groups did, as well, engage external resources for such tasks as training in STS theory, team-building and problem-solving skills.

We learned, then, that there do exist certain methodologies or processes that we can adopt in our efforts to restructure work. STS analysis, a systematic approach to organizational analysis, is one of the better established and validated methods. STS analysis can be successfully undertaken by workers and it can thereby serve to improve organizational effectiveness. It acts as a dynamic and potent instrument for enhancing the work place. Workers can and should participate in the analysis, the design, and the implementation but, only rarely, do they do so in the evaluation of STS projects. Workers possess vital technical and social knowledge needed for effective redesign efforts. Likewise, worker participation gives both a powerful justification for the resulting recommendations and "provides the organization with a memory of the reasons behind the [re] design" (Taylor 1981).

The applicability of STS analysis is not confined to North America and Europe. As a methodology it has generalized or universal validity and is, as such, neither geographically nor culturally delimited. It can illuminate many contexts, in the developed or developing worlds.

Our QWL efforts can no longer be confined to experimentation but must now form the nucleus of an organizational strategy. Only then will QWL be institutionalized; only then will learning and diffusion continuously occur.[4]

We must take a process view, recognizing both the internal and external social systems. Management must display a positive attitude to change and must be prepared to engage all the stakeholders in the process of strategy implementation. The practices presented at the QWL and the 80s Conference serve to reinforce the precept that we can learn by and from doing. By participating in some form of design or implementation process, we are able to invent our own local theory and make our own particular choices. While we can learn much from others, "we must be prepared to reinvent the wheel" (Butteriss 1981), so that our designs are contextually appropriate. Our view must all the while remain systemic, one through which the many complex relationships and meanings of the work place can be perceived.

We also learned from these six cases that the designs resulting from our efforts, though very different, are all fragile. They require constant invigoration. They are deeply socially embedded and require constant vigilance if they are to be free from racism and sexism. They are thus inherently political organizations. They must be systematically and ethically planned so that they can serve as an authentic and exquisite alternative paradigm of work and life.

NOTES

1. From a session at QWL and the 80s entitled "What Do We Mean By Redesign?" with Lyman Ketchum (L. D. Ketchum Associates, USA), Eric Trist (University of Pennsylvania, USA and York University, Canada), and William Westley (McGill University, Canada).

2. From a session at QWL and the 80s entitled "How Do You Get Started—Sherex Chemical Co. Inc." with James Berry, Kenneth Johnson, and Bob Morrison (all of Sherex

Chemical Co. Inc., USA), and Edsel Jones (Oil, Chemical and Atomic Workers International Union, USA).

3. From a session at QWL and the 80s entitled "Congruent Structures—Evaluation/Assessment" with Wilts Alexander and Thomas Scott (both of Alexander, Scott and Associates Inc., USA), Thomas Cummings (University of Southern California, USA), Gert Graverson (Technological Institute, Denmark), Anthony Hopwood (Oxford University, England), Marty Kaplan (Shell Canada, Canada), Lisl Klein (Tavistock Institute of Human Relations, England), Susan Mohrman (University of Southern California, USA), Ian Tanner (Manchester Business School, England), and James Taylor (University of California, Los Angeles, USA).

4. From a session at QWL and the 80s entitled "Corporate Strategy for People at Work—The Volvo Experience" with Berth Jönsson (Volvo Group, Sweden).

REFERENCES

These papers were presented at QWL and the 80s, an international conference on the quality of working life, Toronto, Canada, 1981.

Butteriss, Margaret. 1981. "The Organizational and Social Factors Involved in Introducing Office Automation."

Davies, Alan. 1981. "A Strategy for Planning in a Public Service Union."

Johnston, Murray C., and Porter, Nelson D. 1981. "QWL in the Department of National Defence."

Ketchum, Lyman. 1981. "A Sociotechnical Study in a Developing Country."

Olsen, David. 1981. "Approaching QWL in a Large City: San Francisco's Work Improvement Project."

Taylor, James. 1981. "Employee Participation in the Socio-technical Systems Analysis of a Computer Operations Organization."

Index

absenteeism, 38–39
academics and quality of working life, 147, 149
ACOA, 155–56
action learning, 140
action research, 140
Administrative and Clerical Officers Association. *See* ACOA
agencies, role of, 101–2
ALCOA, 3, 15–16
alienation, 30–31; symptoms of, 27
Aluminum Corporation of America. *See* ALCOA
American Telephone and Telegraph. *See* AT&T
Arden House, first international conference on QWL, v, 88, 97–98
Argyris, Chris, 9
assembly lines, 8, 10, 29
AT&T, 3, 13, 61, 144
Australia: future of society, 120–21; survey of workers, 120–21
automation, 65, 144. *See also* information technology; microprocessing revolution
autonomy. *See* groups, semiautonomous

barefoot social scientist, 152, 153 (note 5)

batch-processing, 56
batch production, 29
Bion, W. R., 149
Bluestone, Irving, vi, 23
boredom, 10, 20
buffers and buffer zones, 19, 28–29
bureaucratization, 116
Burns, Scott, 122
Butteriss, Margaret, 158, 165

Camens, Sam, 24
Canada, Department of National Defence, 160–62
Canadian Labour Congress, 24
causal texture of the environment, 140
change: in organizations, 92–93; management of, 94–95; resistance to, 93–95, 124, 164; social, 33–34; system, 118–19
clerical work, quality of working life in, 159–60. *See also* office automation
codetermination, 45–46; Swedish law of, 25–26
Cohen-Rosenthal, Edward, 25
collective bargaining: in Canada, Department of National Defence, 160–61; and quality of working life, 39, 49, 144–45. *See also* unions, and quality of working life

About the Editors

HANS VAN BEINUM is Executive Director of the Ontario Quality of Working Life Centre in Toronto. He holds a B.A. Hons. degree in Sociology and a D.Litt. in Social Psychology from the University of Groningen. Dr. van Beinum has been involved in developing action research, field experiments, and other QWL approaches and programs for more than 20 years in numerous organizations in Europe, India, and North America.

He was a senior social scientist at the Tavistock Institute of Human Relations in London from 1963 to 1970 and was chairman of the Human Relations Resource Centre of the Tavistock Institute. In 1967 Dr. van Beinum was appointed Professor of Social Psychology for the Foundation for Business Administration at the Netherlands School of Economics in Rotterdam (now called Erasmus University) till his move to Canada in 1978. He was dean of the Foundation for Business Administration from 1970–73. From 1970–77 he was vice-president of the European Institute for Advances Studies in Management in Brussels.

Dr. van Beinum is a member of the Tavistock Institute of Human Relations, London, and a Consulting Associate of the Niagara Institute. He was a member of the executive committee of the former International Council for the Quality of Working Life.

HARVEY KOLODNY is an associate professor in the Faculty of Management Studies at the University of Toronto. His research interests are in the area of organization theory and the design of complex organizations, particularly matrix organization forms. In the last few years those research interests have included sociotechnical systems theory and the quality of working life. Dr. Kolodny is an electronics engineering graduate from McGill University. He has worked as a design, manufacturing, and control systems engineer in high technology engineering industries in Canada, the United Kingdom, and the United States over a period of 15 years. He received an M.B.A. degree from the University of Sherbrooke in Québec and a doctoral degree from the Harvard Business School. Dr. Kolodny's current research is centered in Sweden, Canada, and the United States and focuses on the design process used to develop new plants that are based on a sociotechnical systems theory philosophy.

List of Contributors
and Affiliations

DAVID JENKINS: writer and consultant on industrial relations and QWL, living in Paris, France.

IRVING BLUESTONE: university professor of labor studies, Wayne State University, Michigan; retired vice-president, International Union, United Auto Workers.

ERIC TRIST: professor of organizational behavior and social ecology, Faculty of Environmental Studies, York University, Toronto; professor emeritus, Wharton School, University of Pennsylvania.

RICHARD WALTON: professor of business administration, Harvard University, Boston.

LOUIS E. DAVIS: professor of organizational sciences, Graduate School of Management, University of California, Los Angeles.

ALBERT B. CHERNS: head of Department of Social Sciences, University of Loughborough, England.

EINAR THORSRUD: professor, Work Research Institute, Oslo.

FRED EMERY: first visiting Busch Professor of the Social Systems Science Department, Wharton School, University of Pennsylvania.

ANN ARMSTRONG: Ph.D. candidate, Faculty of Management Studies, University of Toronto.

DATE DUE

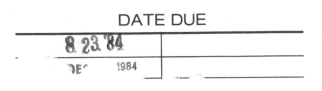

8 23 '84	
DEC 1984